SIMON ARMITAGE

# Paper Aeroplane

Selected Poems

1989–2014

FABER & FABER

First published in 2014
by Faber & Faber Ltd
Bloomsbury House
74–77 Great Russell Street
London WC1B 3DA

This paperback edition first published in 2015

Typeset by RefineCatch Ltd, Bungay, Suffolk
Printed and bound in England by CPI Group (UK) Ltd, Croydon, CR0 4YY

The right of Simon Armitage to be identified as author of
this work has been asserted in accordance with Section 77
of the Copyright, Designs and Patents Act 1988

A CIP record for this book
is available from the British Library

ISBN 978-0-571-31069-2

The author gratefully acknowledges the publishers of the following
publications where some of these poems first appeared:

*Zoom!* (Bloodaxe Books, 1989)
*Xanadu* (Bloodaxe Books, 1992)
*Out of the Blue* (Enitharmon Press, 2008)
*The Not Dead* (Pomona Books, 2008)
*Black Roses* (Pomona Books, 2012)
*Stanza Stones* (Enitharmon Press, 2013)

FSC
www.fsc.org
MIX
Paper from
responsible sources
FSC® C013604

# Contents

# PAPER AEROPLANE

*from* ZOOM!

# Snow Joke

Heard the one about the guy from Heaton Mersey?
Wife at home, lover in Hyde, mistress
in Newton-le-Willows and two pretty girls
in the top grade at Werneth prep. Well,

he was late and he had a good car so he snubbed
the police warning-light and tried to finesse
the last six miles of moorland blizzard,
and the story goes he was stuck within minutes.

So he sat there thinking about life and things;
what the dog does when it catches its tail
and about the snake that ate itself to death.
And he watched the windscreen filling up

with snow, and it felt good, and the whisky
from his hip-flask was warm and smooth.
And of course, there isn't a punchline
but the ending goes something like this:

they found him slumped against the steering wheel
with VOLVO printed backwards in his frozen brow.
And they fought in the pub over hot toddies
as to who was to take the most credit.

Him who took the aerial to be a hawthorn twig?
Him who figured out the contour of his car?
Or him who said he heard the horn, moaning
softly like an alarm clock under an eiderdown?

# It Ain't What You Do It's What It Does to You

I have not bummed across America
with only a dollar to spare, one pair
of busted Levi's and a bowie knife.
I have lived with thieves in Manchester.

I have not padded through the Taj Mahal,
barefoot, listening to the space between
each footfall picking up and putting down
its print against the marble floor. But I

skimmed flat stones across Black Moss on a day
so still I could hear each set of ripples
as they crossed. I felt each stone's momentum
spend itself against the water; then sink.

I have not toyed with a parachute chord
while perched on the lip of a light aircraft;
but I held the wobbly head of a boy
at the day centre, and stroked his fat hands.

And I guess that the tightness in the throat
and the tiny cascading sensation
somewhere inside us are both part of that
sense of something else. That feeling, I mean.

# The Bears in Yosemite Park

are busy in the trash cans, grubbing for toothpaste
but the weather on Mam Tor has buckled the road
into Castleton. A crocodile of hikers spills out
into a distant car park as the rain permeates

our innermost teeshirts, and quickly we realise:
this moment is one which will separate some part
of our lives from another. We will always remember
the mobile of seagulls treading water over Edale.

Killer whales pair for life;

they are calling across the base of the ocean
as we sprint for the shelter of the Blue John mine.
We know the routine. In the furthest cavern
the lights go out and the guide will remind us

that this is true darkness and these splashes
of orange and bristling purple fibre are nothing
but the echoes of light still staining our eyelids.
Back in the car we peel off our sticky layers

and the stacks of rain

are still collapsing sideways as we gear down into
Little Hayfield Please Drive Carefully. On the radio
somebody explains. The bears in Yosemite Park
are stumbling home, legged up with fishing-line

and polythene and above the grind of his skidoo
a ranger curses the politics of skinny-dipping.
This is life. Killer whales are nursing their dead
into quiet waters and we are driving home

in boxer-shorts and bare feet.

# Phenomenology

Harold Garfinkel can go fuck himself.
This is a ten pound note. These are the keys
to your mother's car, and my father's suit
is nicely one half-size too big for me.

The tyres burst the puddles and the lamplight
spills like a moment from the past, only
to settle backwards, become distant and
still further distant in the long darkness

behind. Always we are moving away.
In the tunnel we test the echo of
the engine and check our haircuts in the
rain-spattered quarter-light. Someday, something

will give. When the sun comes up tomorrow
it will dawn on us. But for now we shine
like the stars we understand: I think I'm
Tom Courtenay; you think I'm Billy Liar.

# Don't Blink

Because the six-year-old on the pavilion steps
keeps stepping out of her mother's sling-back sandals
and a jogger on the road has barely enough breath
to say 'It never gets any easier, just quicker'
to his brother who is hoisting a double baby-buggy

over the narrow gate. Other things we can take
or leave: the ambulance that stubs its shock absorbers
on the sleeping policeman; the incensed batsman walking
back towards the bowler, saying if he does that again
he'll ram this steel-sprung Duncan Fearnley down his throat

or through the windscreen of his Ford Fiesta.
Not that this match could be close or anything;
the home team only have nine men and one of those
is the scorer's friend, who at a sensitive age looks
ridiculous in blue shorts and his sister's jumper.

Don't blink. You might miss the perfect smile
of a boy whistling 'Summertime' who has to stop
when he gets to the bit that goes 'Your daddy's rich'
or the man with a dog who turns to ask his friend
why they can't make aeroplanes out of the same stuff

they make black-box flight recorders out of.
You might not even notice that an evening breeze
which wafts the drone of a moorland rescue helicopter
across the field from a mile away, is the same breeze
that chafes the tip from a pile of sawdust

and rocks the jumper of the left-arm spinner, mislaid
for the moment, on the handle of the heavy roller.
The fight in the beer tent hardly gets a mention.
When the light fades, the swifts say more about the weather
than a poet ever could, picking up the smallest insects

dangerously close to the ground.

## Poem

Frank O'Hara was open on the desk
but I went straight for the directory.
Nick was out, Joey was engaged, Jim was
just making coffee and why didn't I

come over. I had Astrud Gilberto
singing 'Bim Bom' on my Sony Walkman
and the sun was drying the damp slates on
the rooftops. I walked in without ringing

and he still wasn't dressed or shaved when we
topped up the coffee with his old man's scotch
(it was only half ten but what the hell)
and took the newspapers into the porch.

Talking Heads were on the radio. I
was just about to mention the football
when he said 'Look, will you help me clear her
wardrobe out?' I said 'Sure Jim, anything.'

# A Painted Bird for Thomas Szasz

It was his anorak that first attracted me.
The foam lining was hanging from a split seam
and a tear that ran the length of his back was patched
with sellotape and sticking plaster. So I watched
as he flitted between the front seats of the bus
and fingered the synthetic fur around his hood.

The next time I noticed was at the terminus
where he was pretending to direct the buses.
From then there was a catalogue of incidents,
moments and locations where we coincided,
and each time I watched him talking to the drivers
who ignored him, and jotting down the route numbers.

One particular time he was in the arcade
eyeing the intricacy of a timetable.
He caught me watching the reflection of his face
so he exhaled onto the surface of the glass
and wrote his name on it. Billy. I passed by him,
breathing in, and he smelt like a wet dog, drying.

Another time I noticed more than I meant to
was a lunchtime at the Probation Day Centre
when I squinted through the gap in the serving hatch
to see him watching the traffic on the bypass.
His focus settled on a simple bicycle
which he followed till it slipped below the skyline.

I also saw him, once, in the covered precinct
pissing himself through his pants onto the concrete
and fumbling with the zip on his anorak.
He bothered me, and later I had to walk back
across where the dark circle of his stain had grown
and was still growing, slowly, outward, like a town.

# November

We walk to the ward from the badly parked car
with your grandma taking four short steps to our two.
We have brought her here to die and we know it.

You check her towel, soap and family trinkets,
pare her nails, parcel her in the rough blankets
and she sinks down into her incontinence.

It is time, John. In their pasty bloodless smiles,
in their slack breasts, their stunned brains and their baldness,
and in us, John: we are almost these monsters.

You're shattered. You give me the keys and I drive
through the twilight zone, past the famous station
to your house, to numb ourselves with alcohol.

Inside, we feel the terror of dusk begin.
Outside we watch the evening, failing again,
and we let it happen. We can say nothing.

Sometimes the sun spangles and we feel alive.
One thing we have to get, John, out of this life.

# The Civilians

We signed the lease and knew we were landed.
Our dream house: half farm, half mansion; gardens
announcing every approach, a greenhouse
      with a southern aspect.
      Here the sunlight lasted;
evenings stretched their sunburnt arms towards us,
held us in their palms: gilded us, warmed us.

We studied the view as if we owned it;
noted each change, nodded and condoned it.
We rode with the roof down, and if the days
      overstepped themselves
      then the golden evenings
spread like ointment through the open valleys,
buttered one side of our spotless washing.

Forget the dangers of iron pyrites
or the boy who ran from his mother's farm
to the golden house on the other hill
      which was a pigsty
      taking the sunlight.
This was God's glory. The big wheel had stopped
with our chair rocking sweetly at the summit.

For what we have, or had, we are grateful.
      To say otherwise
      would be bitterness
and we know better than to surrender.
Behind the hen-house the jalopy is snookered:
      its bodywork sound,
      its engine buggered,

but still there is gold: headlights on the road,
the unchewable crusts of our own loaves,
      old leaves the dog drags in.
      Frost is early this autumn.
      Wrapped up like onions
we shuffle out over the frozen ground,
prop up the line where our sheets are flagging.

# The Stuff

We'd heard all the warnings, knew its nicknames.
It arrived in our town by word of mouth
and crackled like wildfire through the grapevine
of gab and gossip. It came from the south

      so we shunned it, naturally,
      sent it to Coventry

and wouldn't have touched it with a bargepole
if it hadn't been at the club one night.
Well, peer group pressure and all that twaddle
so we fussed around it like flies round shite

      and watched,
      and waited

till one kid risked it, stepped up and licked it
and came from every pore in his body.
That clinched it. It snowballed, whirlpooled. Listen,
no one was more surprised than me to be

      cutting it, mixing it,
      snorting and sniffing it

or bulking it up with scouring powder
or chalk, or snuff, or sodium chloride
and selling it under the flyover.
At first we were laughing. It was all right

      to be drinking it, eating it,
      living and breathing it

but things got seedy, people went missing.
One punter surfaced in the ship-canal
having shed a pair of concrete slippers.
Others were bundled in the back of vans

and were quizzed, thumped,
finished off and dumped

or vanished completely like Weldon Kees,
their cars left idle under the rail bridge
with its cryptic hoarding that stumped the police:
'Oldham – Home of the tubular bandage.'

Others were strangled.
Not that it stopped us.

Someone bubbled us. C.I.D. sussed us
and found some on us. It was cut and dried.
They dusted, booked us, cuffed us and pushed us
down to the station and read us our rights.

Possession and supplying:
we had it, we'd had it.

In Court I ambled up and took the oath
and spoke the addict's side of the story.
I said grapevine, bargepole, whirlpool, chloride,
concrete, bandage, station, story. Honest.

# Zoom!

It begins as a house, an end terrace
in this case
    but it will not stop there. Soon it is
an avenue
    which cambers arrogantly past the Mechanics' Institute,
turns left
    at the main road without even looking
and quickly it is
    a town with all four major clearing banks,
a daily paper
    and a football team pushing for promotion.

On it goes, oblivious to the Planning Acts,
the green belts,
    and before we know it it is out of our hands:
city, nation,
    hemisphere, universe, hammering out in all directions
until suddenly,
    mercifully, it is drawn aside through the eye
of a black hole
    and bulleted into a neighbouring galaxy, emerging
smaller and smoother
    than a billiard ball but weighing more than Saturn.

People stop me in the street, badger me
in the check-out queue
    and ask 'What is this, this that is so small
and so very smooth
    but whose mass is greater than the ringed planet?'
It's just words
    I assure them. But they will not have it.

*from* XANADU

§

We thought of Ashfield and imagined trees,
wood smoke, horses and the ricochet of hooves,
a meltwater stream
like milk from the moors,

beehives, bird life, allotments, a breeze.
Like bloodhounds now we track the moment of truth,
by which I mean
the way we choose

to say which quaver tipped the song into a scream,
to pinpoint how the pinprick widened to a bruise
for you, for me.
I'll list the clues:

the so-called ash, the field, the so-called streets
at sixes, sevens, German shepherds in their schools
of threes
and twos,

for peace of mind this baseball bat, for sleep
these tablets and a certain ratio of booze
will count for sheep
and see us through.

We idle now on waiting lists, and dream
of runways, level crossings, traffic queues;
waiting to come clean,
to break the news

of how we live, of what we have seen,
of how it leaves us, and what that proves.
A light goes green
but nobody moves.

*from* KID

# Gooseberry Season

Which reminds me. He appeared
at noon, asking for water. He'd walked from town
after losing his job, leaving a note for his wife and his brother
and locking his dog in the coal bunker.
We made him a bed

and he slept till Monday.
A week went by and he hung up his coat.
Then a month, and not a stroke of work, a word of thanks,
a farthing of rent or a sign of him leaving.
One evening he mentioned a recipe

for smooth, seedless gooseberry sorbet
but by then I was tired of him: taking pocket money
from my boy at cards, sucking up to my wife and on his last
    night
sizing up my daughter. He was smoking my pipe
as we stirred his supper.

Where does the hand become the wrist?
Where does the neck become the shoulder? The watershed
and then the weight, whatever turns up and tips us over that
    razor's edge
between something and nothing, between
one and the other.

I could have told him this
but didn't bother. We ran him a bath
and held him under, dried him off and dressed him
and loaded him into the back of the pick-up.
Then we drove without headlights

to the county boundary,
dropped the tailgate, and after my boy
had been through his pockets we dragged him like a mattress
across the meadow and on the count of four
threw him over the border.

This is not general knowledge, except
in gooseberry season, which reminds me, and at the table
I have been known to raise an eyebrow, or scoop the sorbet
into five equal portions, for the hell of it.
I mention this for a good reason.

# Brassneck

United, mainly,
every odd Saturday,
or White Hart Lane for a worthwhile away game.
Down in the crowds at the grounds where the bread is:
the gold, the plastic,
the cheque-books, the readies,

the biggest fish
or the easiest meat,
or both. Consider that chap we took last week:
we turned him over and walked off the terrace
with a grand exactly
in dog-eared tenners;

takings like that
don't get reported.
Carter, he's a sort of junior partner;
it's two seasons now since we first teamed up
in the Stretford End
in the FA Cup;

it was all United
when I caught him filching
my cigarette case, and he felt me fishing
a prial of credit cards out of his britches.
Since that day
we've worked these pitches.

We tend to kick off
by the hot dog vans
 and we've lightened a good many fair-weather fans
 who haven't a clue where to queue for tickets.
 Anything goes, if it's
 loose we lift it.

At City last year
in the derby match
 we did the right thing with a smart-looking lass
 who'd come unhitched in the crush from her friend.
 We escorted her out
 of the Platt Lane End,

arm in arm
along the touchline,
 past the tunnel and out through the turnstile
 and directed her on to a distant police car.
 I did the talking
 and Carter fleeced her.

As Carter once put it:
when we're on the ball
 we can clean someone out, from a comb to a coil,
 and we need nine eyes to watch for the coppers
 though at Goodison Park
 when I got collared

two bright young bobbies
took me into the toilets
and we split the difference. Bent policemen;
there's always a couple around when you need them.
It's usually Autumn
when we loosen our fingers

at the Charity Shield
which is pretty big business
though semis and finals are birthdays and Christmas.
Hillsborough was a different ball game of course;
we'd started early,
then saw what the score was,

so we turned things in
as a mark of respect,
just kept enough back to meet certain expenses
(I'm referring here to a red and blue wreath;
there are trading standards,
even among thieves).

Carter keeps saying
he'd be quick to wager
that worse things go on in the name of wages,
but I've let Carter know there's a place and a time
to say as we speak,
speak as we find.

Speaking of Carter,
and not that I mind,
he thinks I'm a touch on the gingery side:
my voice a little too tongued and grooved,
my locks a little
too washed and groomed,

my cuticles tenderly
pushed back and pruned,
both thumbnails capped with a full half-moon,
each fingernail manicured, pared and polished . . .
We can work hand in hand if we stick to the rules:
he keeps his cunt-hooks out of my wallet,
I keep my tentacles
out of his pocket.

# The Catch

Forget
the long, smouldering
afternoon. It is

this moment
when the ball scoots
off the edge

of the bat; upwards,
backwards, falling
seemingly

beyond him
yet he reaches
and picks it

out
of its loop
like

an apple
from a branch,
the first of the season.

# You May Turn Over and Begin . . .

'Which of these films was Dirk Bogarde
not in? One hundredweight of bauxite

makes how much aluminium?
How many tales in *The Decameron*?'

General Studies, the upper sixth, a doddle, a cinch
for anyone with an ounce of common sense

or a calculator
with a memory feature.

Having galloped through but not caring enough
to check or double-check, I was dreaming of

milk-white breasts and nakedness, or more specifically
virginity.

That term – everybody felt the heat
but the girls were having none of it:

long and cool like cocktails,
out of reach, their buns and pigtails

only let out for older guys with studded jackets
and motor-bikes and spare helmets.

One jot of consolation
was the tall spindly girl riding pillion

on her man's new Honda,
who, with the lights at amber,

put down both feet and stood to stretch her limbs,
to lift the visor and push back her fringe

and to smooth her tight jeans.
As he pulled off down the street

she stood there like a wishbone,
high and dry, legs wide open,

and rumour has it he didn't notice
till he came round in the ambulance

having underbalanced on a tight left-hander.
*A Taste of Honey*. Now I remember.

## At Sea

It is not through weeping,
but all evening the pale blue eye
on your most photogenic side has kept
its own unfathomable tide. Like the boy
at the dyke I have been there:

held out a huge finger,
lifted atoms of dust with the point
of a tissue and imagined slivers of hair
in the oil on the cornea. We are both
in the dark, but I go on

drawing the eyelid up by its lashes,
folding it almost inside-out, then finding
and hiding every mirror in the house
as the iris, besieged with the ink
of blood rolls back

into its own orbit. Nothing
will help it. Through until dawn
you dream the true story of the boy
who hooked out his eye and ate it,
so by six in the morning

I am steadying the ointment
that will bite like an onion, piping
a line of cream while avoiding the pupil
and in no time it is glued shut
like a bad mussel.

Friends call round
and mean well. They wait
and whisper in the air-lock of the lobby
with patches, eyewash, the truth
about mascara.

Even the cats are on to it;
they bring in starlings, and because their feathers
are the colours of oil on water in sunlight
they are a sign of something.
In the long hours

beyond us, irritations heal
into arguments. For the eighteenth time
it comes to this: the length of your leg sliding out
from the covers, the ball of your foot
like a fist on the carpet

while downstairs
I cannot bring myself to hear it.
Words have been spoken, things that were bottled
have burst open and to walk in now
would be to walk in

on the ocean.

# Poem

And if it snowed and snow covered the drive
he took a spade and tossed it to one side.
And always tucked his daughter up at night.
And slippered her the one time that she lied.

And every week he tipped up half his wage.
And what he didn't spend each week he saved.
And praised his wife for every meal she made.
And once, for laughing, punched her in the face.

And for his mum he hired a private nurse.
And every Sunday taxied her to church.
And he blubbed when she went from bad to worse.
And twice he lifted ten quid from her purse.

Here's how they rated him when they looked back:
sometimes he did this, sometimes he did that.

# Kid

Batman, big shot, when you gave the order
to grow up, then let me loose to wander
leeward, freely through the wild blue yonder
as you liked to say, or ditched me, rather,
in the gutter . . . well, I turned the corner.
Now I've scotched that 'he was like a father
to me' rumour, sacked it, blown the cover
on that 'he was like an elder brother'
story, let the cat out on that caper
with the married woman, how you took her
downtown on expenses in the motor.
Holy robin-redbreast-nest-egg-shocker!
Holy roll-me-over-in-the-clover,
I'm not playing ball boy any longer
Batman, now I've doffed that off-the-shoulder
Sherwood-Forest-green and scarlet number
for a pair of jeans and crew-neck jumper;
now I'm taller, harder, stronger, older.
Batman, it makes a marvellous picture:
you without a shadow, stewing over
chicken giblets in the pressure cooker,
next to nothing in the walk-in larder,
punching the palm of your hand all winter,
you baby, now I'm the real boy wonder.

# Great Sporting Moments: The Treble

The rich! I love them. Trust them to suppose
the gift of tennis is deep in their bones.

Those chaps from the coast with all their own gear
from electric eyes to the umpire's chair,

like him whose arse I whipped with five choice strokes
perfected on West Yorkshire's threadbare courts:

a big first serve that strained his alloy frame,
a straight return that went back like a train,

a lob that left him gawping like a fish,
a backhand pass that kicked and drew a wisp

of chalk, a smash like a rubber bullet
and a bruise to go with it. Three straight sets.

Smarting in the locker rooms he offered
double or quits; he was a born golfer

and round the links he'd wipe the floor with me.
I played the ignoramus to a tee:

the pleb in the gag who asked the viscount
what those eggcup-like things were all about –

'They're to rest my balls on when I'm driving.'
'Blimey, guv, Rolls-Royce think of everything' –

but at the fifth when I hadn't faltered
he lost his rag and threw down the gauntlet;

we'd settle this like men: with the gloves on.
I said no, no, no, no, no, no, no. OK, come on then.

## Not the Furniture Game

His hair was a crow fished out of a blocked chimney
and his eyes were boiled eggs with the tops hammered in
and his blink was a cat flap
and his teeth were bluestones or Easter Island statues
and his bite was a perfect horseshoe.
His nostrils were both barrels of a shotgun, loaded.
And his mouth was an oil exploration project gone bankrupt
and his last smile was a Caesarean section
and his tongue was an iguanodon
and his whistle was a laser beam
and his laugh was a bad case of kennel cough.
He coughed, and it was malt whisky.
And his headaches were Arson in Her Majesty's Dockyards
and his arguments were outboard motors strangled with
    fishing line
and his neck was a bandstand
and his Adam's apple was a ballcock
and his arms were milk running off from a broken bottle.
His elbows were boomerangs or pinking shears.
And his wrists were ankles
and his handshakes were puff adders in the bran tub
and his fingers were astronauts found dead in their spacesuits
and the palms of his hands were action paintings
and both thumbs were blue touchpaper.
And his shadow was an opencast mine.
And his dog was a sentry-box with no one in it
and his heart was a First World War grenade discovered by
    children
and his nipples were timers for incendiary devices

and his shoulder-blades were two butchers at the meat-cleaving
    competition
and his belly-button was the Falkland Islands
and his private parts were the Bermuda Triangle
and his backside was a priest hole
and his stretchmarks were the tide going out.
The whole system of his blood was Dutch elm disease.
And his legs were depth charges
and his knees were fossils waiting to be tapped open
and his ligaments were rifles wrapped in oilcloth under the
    floorboards
and his calves were the undercarriages of Shackletons.
The balls of his feet were where meteorites had landed
and his toes were a nest of mice under the lawnmower.
And his footprints were Vietnam
and his promises were hot-air balloons floating off over
    the trees
and his one-liners were footballs through other people's
    windows
and his grin was the Great Wall of China as seen from
    the moon
and the last time they talked, it was apartheid.

She was a chair, tipped over backwards
with his donkey jacket on her shoulders.

They told him,
and his face was a hole
where the ice had not been thick enough to hold her.

## Robinson's Resignation

Because I am done with this thing called work,
the paperclips and staples of it all.
The customers and their huge excuses,
their incredulous lies and their beautiful
foul-mouthed daughters. I am swimming with it,
right up to here with it. And I am bored,
bored like the man who married a mermaid.

And I am through with the business of work.
In meetings, with the minutes, I have dreamed
and doodled, drifted away then undressed
and dressed almost every single woman,
every button, every zip and buckle.
For eighteen months in this diving-helmet
I have lived with the stench of my own breath.

So I am finished with the whole affair.
As for this friendship thing, I couldn't give
a weeping fig for those so-called brothers
who are all voltage, no current. I have
emptied my locker. I should like to leave
and to fold things now like a pair of gloves
or two clean socks, one into the other.

This is my final word. Nothing will follow.

## About His Person

Five pounds fifty in change, exactly,
a library card on its date of expiry.

A postcard, stamped,
unwritten, but franked,

a pocket-size diary slashed with a pencil
from March twenty-fourth to the first of April.

A brace of keys for a mortise lock,
an analogue watch, self-winding, stopped.

A final demand
in his own hand,

a rolled-up note of explanation
planted there like a spray carnation

but beheaded, in his fist.
A shopping list.

A giveaway photograph stashed in his wallet,
a keepsake banked in the heart of a locket.

No gold or silver,
but crowning one finger

a ring of white unweathered skin.
That was everything.

*from* BOOK OF MATCHES

★

Mother, any distance greater than a single span
requires a second pair of hands.
You come to help me measure windows, pelmets, doors,
the acres of the walls, the prairies of the floors.

You at the zero-end, me with the spool of tape, recording
length, reporting metres, centimetres back to base, then leaving
up the stairs, the line still feeding out, unreeling
years between us. Anchor. Kite.

I space-walk through the empty bedrooms, climb
the ladder to the loft, to breaking point, where something
has to give;
two floors below your fingertips still pinch
the last one-hundredth of an inch . . . I reach
towards a hatch that opens on an endless sky
to fall or fly.

★

My father thought it bloody queer,
the day I rolled home with a ring of silver in my ear
half hidden by a mop of hair. 'You've lost your head.
If that's how easily you're led
you should've had it through your nose instead.'

And even then I hadn't had the nerve to numb
the lobe with ice, then drive a needle through the skin,
then wear a safety-pin. It took a jeweller's gun
to pierce the flesh, and then a friend
to thread a sleeper in, and where it slept
the hole became a sore, became a wound, and wept.

At twenty-nine, it comes as no surprise to hear
my own voice breaking like a tear, released like water,
cried from way back in the spiral of the ear. *If I were you,*
*I'd take it out and leave it out next year.*

★

I am very bothered when I think
of the bad things I have done in my life.
Not least that time in the chemistry lab
when I held a pair of scissors by the blades
and played the handles
in the naked lilac flame of the Bunsen burner;
then called your name, and handed them over.

O the unrivalled stench of branded skin
as you slipped your thumb and middle finger in,
then couldn't shake off the two burning rings. Marked,
the doctor said, for eternity.

Don't believe me, please, if I say
that was just my butterfingered way, at thirteen,
of asking you if you would marry me.

★

I'm dreaming of that work, *Man Seated Reading
at a Table in a Lofty Room*, and while I sleep
a virus sweeps the earth, and when I wake I see
the population of the world is

me.

I take the observation suite in Emley Moor mast
to watch the skyline from the Appalachians to the Alps;
those signs of life, a thousand miles away perhaps,
are nothing more than fireflies nesting in the grass
across the heath.

I manage very well, become a master in the arts
of food and drink and heat and light,
but then at night, with no one in the world
to cut my throat, I lock and latch
and bar and bolt the windows and the hatch.

★

Those bastards in their mansions:
to hear them shriek, you'd think
I'd poisoned the dogs and vaulted the ditches,
crossed the lawns in stocking feet and threadbare britches,
forced the door of one of the porches, and lifted
the gift of fire from the burning torches,

then given heat and light to streets and houses,
told the people how to ditch their cuffs and shackles,
armed them with the iron from their wrists and ankles.

Those lords and ladies in their palaces and castles,
they'd have me sniffed out by their beagles,
picked at by their eagles, pinned down, grilled
beneath the sun.

Me, I stick to the shadows, carry a gun.

★

æŋkɪˈləʊzɪŋ spɒndɪˈlaɪtɪs:
ankylosing meaning bond or join,
and spondylitis meaning of the bone or spine.
That half explains the cracks and clicks,
the clockwork of my joints and discs,
the ratchet of my hips. I'm fossilising –
every time I rest
I let the gristle knit, weave, mesh.

My dear, my skeleton will set like biscuit overnight,
like glass, like ice, and you can choose
to snap me back to life before first light,
or let me laze until
the shape I take becomes the shape I keep.

Don't leave me be. Don't let me sleep.

★

I've made out a will; I'm leaving myself
to the National Health. I'm sure they can use
the jellies and tubes and syrups and glues,
the web of nerves and veins, the loaf of brains,
an assortment of fillings and stitches and wounds,
blood – a gallon exactly of bilberry soup –
the chassis or cage or cathedral of bone;
but not the heart, they can leave that alone.

They can have the lot, the whole stock:
the loops and coils and sprockets and springs and rods,
the twines and cords and strands,
the face, the case, the cogs and the hands,

but not the pendulum, the ticker;
leave that where it stops or hangs.

★

No convictions – that's my one major fault.
Nothing to tempt me to scream and shout, nothing
to raise Cain or make a song and dance about.

A man like me could be a real handful,
steeping himself overnight in petrol,
becoming inflamed on behalf of the world,
letting his blood boil, letting his hair curl.

I have a beauty spot three inches south-east
of my nose, a heart that has to be a match
for any pocket watch, a fist
that opens like a fine Swiss Army knife,
and certain tricks that have been known
to bring about spontaneous applause.
But no cause, no cause.

## The Lost Letter of the Late Jud Fry

Wake.
And in my head
walk barefoot, naked from the bed
towards the day, then
wait.

Hold.
The dawn will crack
its egg into the morning's bowl
and him on horseback,
gold.

Me,
I'm in the shed, I'm
working on it: a plus b plus c, it's
you, him, me. It's
three.

Hell,
this hole, this shack.
The sun makes light of me
behind my back.
Well,

good.
I give you the applause
of ringdoves lifting from the wood
and, for an encore,
blood.

Look,
see, no man
should be me, the very opposite
of snowman:
soot.

I
work that black dust
where I slice your name into my forearm
with a jackknife: L.A.U.R.E.
Y.

You
at the window now,
undressed. I underestimated him,
never saw you as a pair, a
two.

Yours –
that's him for sure.
The sun will have its day,
its weeks, months,
years.

Fine.
But just for once, for me,
dig deep, think twice, be otherwise, be
someone else this time.
Mine.

# Parable of the Dead Donkey

Instructions arrived by registered post
under cover of separate envelopes:
directions first
to pinpoint the place
in the shape of maps and compass bearings;
those, then forms and stamps for loss of earnings.
So much was paid
to diggers of graves
by keepers or next of kin, per leg
(which made for the dumping of quadrupeds):
sixteen quid
to send off a pig
or sink a pit for a dog or pony.
But less to plant a man than a donkey.
Cheaper by half
for a pregnant horse
that died with all four hooves inside her
than one with a stillborn foal beside her.
And this was a bind,
being duty bound
where ownership was unestablished.
We filled the flasks and loaded the Transit,
then set out, making
for the undertaking.

Facing north, he was dead at three o'clock
in a ring of meadow grass, closely cropped,
where a metal chain
on a wooden stake
had stopped him ambling off at an angle,

worn him down in a perfect circle.
We burrowed in
right next to him
through firm white soil. An hour's hard labour
took us five feet down – and then the weather:
thunder biting
the heels of lightning,
a cloudburst drawing a curtain of rain
across us, filling the bath of the grave,
and we waded in it
for one more minute,
dredged and shovelled as the tide was rising,
bailed out for fear of drowning, capsizing.
Back on top
we weighed him up,
gave some thought to this beast of the Bible:
the nose and muzzle, the teeth, the eyeballs,
the rump, the hindquarters,
the flanks, the shoulders,
everything soothed in the oil of the rain –
the eel of his tongue, the keel of his spine,
the rope of his tail,
the weeds of his mane.
Then we turned him about and slipped his anchor,
eased him out of the noose of his tether,
and rolled him in
and started to dig.
But even with donkey, water and soil
there wasn't enough to level the hole
after what was washed away

or turned into clay
or trodden in, so we opened the earth
and started in on a second trench for dirt
to fill the first.
Which left a taste
of starting something that wouldn't finish:
a covered grave with a donkey in it,
a donkey-size hole
within a stone's throw
and not a single bone to drop in it
or a handful of dust to toss on top of it.

The van wouldn't start, so we wandered home
on foot, in the dark, without supper or profit.

# Hitcher

I'd been tired, under
the weather, but the ansaphone kept screaming:
*One more sick-note, mister, and you're finished. Fired.*
I thumbed a lift to where the car was parked.
A Vauxhall Astra. It was hired.

I picked him up in Leeds.
He was following the sun to west from east
with just a toothbrush and the good earth for a bed. The truth,
he said, was blowin' in the wind,
or round the next bend.

I let him have it
on the top road out of Harrogate – once
with the head, then six times with the krooklok
in the face – and didn't even swerve.
I dropped it into third

and leant across
to let him out, and saw him in the mirror
bouncing off the kerb, then disappearing down the verge.
We were the same age, give or take a week.
He'd said he liked the breeze

to run its fingers
through his hair. It was twelve noon.
The outlook for the day was moderate to fair.
Stitch that, I remember thinking,
you can walk from there.

## To His Lost Lover

Now they are no longer
any trouble to each other

he can turn things over, get down to that list
of things that never happened, all of the lost

unfinishable business.
For instance . . . for instance,

how he never clipped and kept her hair, or drew a hairbrush
through that style of hers, and never knew how not to blush

at the fall of her name in close company.
How they never slept like buried cutlery –

two spoons or forks cupped perfectly together –
or made the most of some heavy weather,

walked out into hard rain under sheet lightning,
or did the gears while the other was driving.

How he never raised his fingertips
to stop the segments of her lips

from breaking the news,
or tasted the fruit,

or picked for himself the pear of her heart,
or lifted her hand to where his own heart

[63]

was a small, dark, terrified bird
in her grip. Where it hurt.

Or said the right thing,
or put it in writing.

And never fled the black mile back to his house
before midnight, or coaxed another button of her blouse,

then another,
or knew her

favourite colour,
her taste, her flavour,

and never ran a bath or held a towel for her,
or soft-soaped her, or whipped her hair

into an ice-cream cornet or a beehive
of lather, or acted out of turn, or misbehaved

when he might have, or worked a comb
where no comb had been, or walked back home

through a black mile hugging a punctured heart,
where it hurt, where it hurt, or helped her hand

to his butterfly heart
in its two blue halves.

And never almost cried,
and never once described

an attack of the heart,
or under a silk shirt

nursed in his hand her breast,
her left, like a tear of flesh

wept by the heart,
where it hurts,

or brushed with his thumb the nut of her nipple,
or drank intoxicating liquors from her navel.

Or christened the Pole Star in her name,
or shielded the mask of her face like a flame,

a pilot light,
or stayed the night,

or steered her back to that house of his,
or said 'Don't ask me to say how it is

I like you.
I just might do.'

How he never figured out a fireproof plan,
or unravelled her hand, as if her hand

were a solid ball
of silver foil

and discovered a lifeline hiding inside it,
and measured the trace of his own alongside it.

But said some things and never meant them –
sweet nothings anybody could have mentioned.

And left unsaid some things he should have spoken,
about the heart, where it hurt exactly, and how often.

*from* THE DEAD SEA POEMS

FOR THE DEAD SEA POEMS

# Man with a Golf Ball Heart

They set about him with a knife and fork, I heard,
and spooned it out. Dunlop, dimpled, perfectly hard.
It bounced on stone but not on softer ground – they made
a note of that. They slit the skin – a leathery,
rubbery, eyelid thing – and further in, three miles
of gut or string, elastic. Inside that, a pouch
or sac of pearl-white balm or gloss, like Copydex.
It weighed in at the low end of the litmus test
but wouldn't burn, and tasted bitter, bad, resin
perhaps from a tree or plant. And it gave off gas
that caused them all to weep when they inspected it.

That heart had been an apple once, they reckoned. Green.
They had a scheme to plant an apple there again
beginning with a pip, but he rejected it.

# I Say I Say I Say

Anyone here had a go at themselves
for a laugh? Anyone opened their wrists
with a blade in the bath? Those in the dark
at the back, listen hard. Those at the front
in the know, those of us who have, hands up,
let's show that inch of lacerated skin
between the forearm and the fist. Let's tell it
like it is: strong drink, a crimson tidemark
round the tub, a yard of lint, white towels
washed a dozen times, still pink. Tough luck.
A passion then for watches, bangles, cuffs.
A likely story: you were lashed by brambles
picking berries from the woods. Come clean, come good,
repeat with me the punchline 'Just like blood'
when those at the back rush forward to say
how a little love goes a long long long way.

# Before You Cut Loose,

                                        put dogs on the list
of difficult things to lose. Those dogs ditched
on the North York Moors or the Sussex Downs
or hurled like bags of sand from rented cars
have followed their noses to market towns
and bounced like balls into their owners' arms.
I heard one story of a dog that swam
to the English coast from the Isle of Man,
and a dog that carried eggs and bacon
and a morning paper from the village
surfaced umpteen leagues and two years later,
bacon eaten but the eggs unbroken,
newsprint dry as tinder, to the letter.
A dog might wander the width of the map
to bury its head in its owner's lap,
crawl the last mile to dab a bleeding paw
against its own front door. To die at home,
a dog might walk its four legs to the bone.
You can take off the tag and the collar
but a dog wears one coat and one colour.
A dog got rid of – that's a dog for life.
No dog howls like a dog kicked out at night.
Try looking a dog like that in the eye.

# Goalkeeper with a Cigarette

That's him in the green, green cotton jersey,
prince of the clean sheets – some upright insect
boxed between the sticks, the horizontal
and the pitch, stood with something up his sleeve,
armed with a pouch of tobacco and skins
to roll his own, or else a silver tin
containing eight or nine already rolled.
That's him with one behind his ear, between
his lips, or one tucked out of sight and lit –
a stamen cupped in the bud of his fist.
That's him sat down, not like those other clowns,
performing acrobatics on the bar, or press-ups
in the box, or running on the spot,
togged out in turtleneck pyjama-suits
with hands as stunted as a bunch of thumbs,
hands that are bandaged or swaddled with gloves,
laughable, frying-pan, sausage-man gloves.
Not my man, though, that's not what my man does;
a man who stubs his reefers on the post
and kicks his heels in the stud-marks and butts,
lighting the next from the last, in one breath
making the save of the year with his legs,
taking back a deep drag on the goal-line
in the next; on the one hand throwing out
or snaffling the ball from a high corner,
flicking off loose ash with the other. Or
in the freezing cold with both teams snorting
like flogged horses, with captains and coaches
effing and jeffing at backs and forwards,
talking steam, screaming exhausting orders,

that's not breath coming from my bloke, it's smoke.
Not him either goading the terraces,
baring his arse to the visitors' end
and dodging the sharpened ten-pence pieces,
playing up, picking a fight, but that's him
cadging a light from the ambulance men,
loosing off smoke rings, zeros or halos
that drift off, passively, over the goals
into nobody's face, up nobody's nose.
He is what he is, does whatever suits him,
because he has no highfalutin song
to sing, no neat message for the nation
on the theme of genius or dedication.
In his passport, under 'occupation',
no one forced the man to print the word
'custodian', and in *The Faber Book*
*of Handy Hints* his five-line entry reads:
'You young pretenders, keepers of the nought,
the nish, defenders of the sweet fuck-all,
think bigger than your pockets, profiles, health;
better by half to take a sideways view,
take a tip from me and deface yourselves.'

# The Two of Us

(after Laycock)

You sat sitting in your country seat
with maidens, servants waiting hand and foot.
You eating swan, crustaceans, starters, seconds, sweet.
You dressed for dinner, worsted, made to measure. Cut:
me darning socks, me lodging at the gate,
me stewing turnips, beet, one spud,
a badger bone. Turf squealing in the grate –
no coal, no wood.

No good. You in your splendour: leather,
rhinestone, ermine, snakeskin, satin, silk,
a felt hat finished with a dodo feather.
Someone's seen you swimming lengths in gold-top milk.
Me parched, me in a donkey jacket,
brewing tea from sawdust mashed in cuckoo spit,
me waiting for the peaks to melt, the rain to racket
on the metal roof, the sky to split,

and you on-stream, piped-up, plugged-in, you worth a mint
and tighter than a turtle's snatch.
Me making light of making do with peat and flint
for heat, a glow-worm for a reading lamp. No match.
The valleys where the game is, where the maize is –
yours. I've got this plot just six foot long
by three foot wide, for greens for now, for daisies
when I'm dead and gone.

You've got the lot, the full set:
chopper, Roller, horse-drawn carriage, microlight, skidoo,
a rosewood yacht, a private jet.
I'm all for saying that you're fucking loaded, you.
And me, I clomp about on foot from field to street;
these clogs I'm shod with, held together now with segs
and fashioned for my father's father's father's feet –
they're on their last legs.

Some in the village reckon we're alike, akin:
same neck, same chin. Up close that's what they've found,
some sameness in the skin,
or else they've tapped me on the back and you've turned round.
Same seed, they say, same shoot,
like I'm some cutting taken from the tree,
like I'm some twig related to the root.
But I can't see it, me.

So when it comes to nailing down the lid
if I were you I wouldn't go with nothing.
Pick some goods and chattels, bits and bobs like Tutankhamen
    did
and have them planted in the coffin.
Opera glasses, fob-watch, fountain pen, a case of fishing flies,
a silver name-tag necklace full-stopped with a precious stone,
a pair of one pound coins to plug the eyes,
a credit card, a mobile phone,

some sentimental piece of earthenware,
a collar stud, a cufflink and a tiepin,
thirteen things to stand the wear and tear
of seasons underground, and I'll take what I'm standing up in.
That way, on the day they dig us out
they'll know that you were something really fucking fine
and I was nowt.
Keep that in mind,

because the worm won't know your make of bone from mine.

*from* MOON COUNTRY

## Song of the West Men

To the far of the far
off the isles of the isles,
near the rocks of the rocks
which the guillemots stripe
with the shite of their shite,

a trawler went down
in the weave of the waves,
and a fisherman swam
for the life of his life
through the swell of the sea

which was one degree C.
And the bones of his bones
were cooler than stone,
and the tide of his blood
was slower than slow.

He met with the land
where the cliffs of the cliffs
were steeper than sheer,
where the sheep had to graze
by the teeth of their teeth.

So he put out again
for the beach,
and made it to lava
that took back his skin
to the feet of his feet,

and arrived at a door
with a tenth of a tale
that was taller than tall,
as cold and as bled as a man
from a fridge. But he lived.

The good of the good
will come this way, they say:
tattered and torn,
unlikely and out of the storm,
if it comes at all.

# Listen Here

It will not be got
from the kernel of rock
where a seismograph samples the murmur of stone,
bugging the pulse where quakes assemble
in swarms and drones.

It will not be caught
in the berth of a boat as it trawls.
Marine life idles in absolute time to starboard and port,
the mid-Atlantic splits its stitches
and the blue whale yawns.

It will not be farmed
in the far of the ground. There,
the wind goes out of its way for somewhere to sound,
unloading the scream of the sea
on the shell of the ear.

It will not be traced
to the deep down of a cave,
where a word on the loose is a bird in a box, a black box;
water clocks the midnight days
in slow, synthesised drops.

It will not be told
by the wide open road.
Chippings tune the forks and spokes of mountain bikes
or station-wagons tread and hold
in four-wheel drive.

It will not be bought
for the price of a long walk
above cliffs. Seabirds needle the air with their beaks,
come close with scraps of talk,
snatches of speech.

It will not be clinched
with equipment, will not be tricked
by holding a microphone out to the air, the water or land
and recording the cracks and clicks
of bones in the hand.

It will not be had,
or fixed. Made of finer stuff,
to find it is to let it come to mind, then bluff,
or lie, or think, or wish.
Now hear this.

*from* CLOUDCUCKOOLAND

# A Glory

Right here you made an angel of yourself,
free-falling backwards into last night's snow,
indenting a straight, neat, crucified shape,
then flapping your arms, one stroke, a great bird,
to leave the impression of wings. It worked.
Then you found your feet, sprang clear of the print
and the angel remained: fixed, countersunk,
open wide, hosting the whole of the sky.

Losing sleep because of it, I backtrack
to the place, out of earshot of the streets,
above the fetch and reach of the town.
The scene of the crime. Five-eighths of the moon.
On ground where snow has given up the ghost
it lies on its own, spread-eagled, embossed,
commending itself, star of its own cause.
Priceless thing – the faceless hood of the head,
grass poking out through the scored spine, the wings
on the turn, becoming feathered, clipped.

Cattle would trample roughshod over it,
hikers might come with pebbles for the eyes,
a choice of fruit for the nose and the lips;
somebody's boy might try it on for size,
might lie down in its shroud, might suit, might fit. Angel,
from under the shade and shelter of trees
I keep watch, wait for the dawn to take you,
raise you, imperceptibly, by degrees.

# The Tyre

Just how it came to rest where it rested,
miles out, miles from the last farmhouse even,
was a fair question. Dropped by hurricane
or aeroplane perhaps for some reason,
put down as a cairn or marker, then lost.
Tractor-size, six or seven feet across,
it was sloughed, unconscious, warm to the touch,
its gashed, rhinoceros, sea-lion skin
nursing a gallon of rain in its gut.
Lashed to the planet with grasses and roots,
it had to be cut. Stood up it was drunk
or slugged, wanted nothing more than to slump,
to spiral back to its circle of sleep,
dream another year in its nest of peat.
We bullied it over the moor, drove it,
pushed from the back or turned it from the side,
unspooling a thread in the shape and form
of its tread, in its length and in its line,
rolled its weight through broken walls, felt the shock
when it met with stones, guided its sleepwalk
down to meadows, fields, onto level ground.
There and then we were one connected thing,
five of us, all hands steering a tall ship
or one hand fingering a coin or ring.

Once on the road it picked up pace, freewheeled,
then moved up through the gears, and wouldn't give
to shoulder-charges, kicks; resisted force
until to tangle with it would have been
to test bone against engine or machine,

to be dragged in, broken, thrown out again
minus a limb. So we let the thing go,
leaning into the bends and corners,
balanced and centred, riding the camber,
carried away with its own momentum.
We pictured an incident up ahead:
life carved open, gardens in half, parted,
a man on a motorbike taken down,
a phone-box upended, children erased,
police and an ambulance in attendance,
scuff-marks and the smell of burning rubber,
the tyre itself embedded in a house
or lying in the gutter, playing dead.
But down in the village the tyre was gone,
and not just gone but unseen and unheard of,
not curled like a cat in the graveyard, not
cornered in the playground like a reptile,
or found and kept like a giant fossil.
Not there or anywhere. No trace. Thin air.

Being more in tune with the feel of things
than science and facts, we knew that the tyre
had travelled too fast for its size and mass,
and broken through some barrier of speed,
outrun the act of being driven, steered,
and at that moment gone beyond itself
towards some other sphere, and disappeared.

# The Winner

When the feeling went in the lower half of my right arm
they fitted a power-tool into the elbow joint
with adjustable heads. When I lost the left
they gave me a ball on a length of skipping-rope
and I played the part of a swingball post
on a summer lawn for a circle of friends.
After the pins and needles in my right leg
they grafted a shooting-stick onto the stump.
When septicaemia took the other peg
I thanked the mysterious ways of the Lord
for the gift of sight and my vocal cords.
With the brush in my teeth, I painted Christmas cards.
When I went blind, they threaded light-bulbs
into the sockets, and slotted a mouth-organ
into the groove of the throat when cancer struck.
For ears, they kitted me out with a baby's sock
for one, and a turned-out pocket, sellotaped on.

Last autumn I managed the Lyke Wake Walk,
forty-odd miles in twenty-four hours – oh Ma,
treasure this badge that belongs to your son
with his nerves of steel and his iron will.
This Easter I'm taking the Life Saving Test – oh Pa,
twenty-five lengths of the baths towing a dead weight,
picture your son in his goggles and vest, with a heart
like a water-pump under a battleship chest.

# For the Record

Ever since the very brutal extraction
of all four of my wisdom teeth,
I've found myself talking
with another man's mouth, so to speak,
and my tongue has become a mollusc
such as an oyster or clam,
broken and entered, licking
its wounds in its shell.

I was tricked into sleep by a man with a smile,
who slipped me the dose
like a great-uncle slipping his favourite nephew
a ten-pound note, like
so, back-handed, then tipped me a wink.
I was out with the stars,
and woke up later, crying,
and wanting to hold the hand of the nurse.

Prior to that, my only experience
under the knife was when I was five,
when my tonsils were hanging
like two bats at the back of a cave
and had to be snipped. But that
was a piece of piss compared with this,
which involved, amongst other things,
three grown men, a monkey-wrench

and the dislocation of my jaw. I wonder,
is this a case of excessive force,
like the powers-that-be evicting
a family of four, dragging them
kicking and screaming, clinging to furniture,
out through their own front door?
Like drawing all four corners of the earth
through the Arc de Triomphe.

You might think that with all the advances
in medical science
teeth like these could be taken out
through the ears or the anus,
or be shattered like kidney stones
by lasers from a safe distance.
But it seems that the art
hasn't staggered too far since the days

when a dentist might set up his stall
at a country fair
or travelling circus.
I'm also reminded of John Henry Small
of Devizes, who put his fist in his mouth
but couldn't spit it out,
and the hand was removed, forthwith,
along with his canines and incisors.

Returning to myself, the consultant says
I should wait another week at least
before saying something in haste
which at leisure I might come to repent.
But my mouth still feels
like a car with its wheels stolen, propped up
on bricks, and I'm unhappy about the way
they stitched the tip of my tongue

to my cheek.

# Homecoming

Think, two things on their own and both at once.
The first, that exercise in trust, where those in front
stand with their arms spread wide and free-fall
backwards, blind, and those behind take all the weight.

The second, one canary-yellow cotton jacket
on a cloakroom floor, uncoupled from its hook,
becoming scuffed and blackened underfoot. Back home
the very model of a model of a mother, yours, puts
two and two together, makes a proper fist of it
and points the finger. Temper, temper. Questions
in the house. You seeing red. Blue murder. Bed.

Then midnight when you slip the latch and sneak
no further than the call-box at the corner of the street;
I'm waiting by the phone, although it doesn't ring
because it's sixteen years or so before we'll meet.
Retrace that walk towards the garden gate; in silhouette
a father figure waits there, wants to set things straight.

These ribs are pleats or seams. These arms are sleeves.
These fingertips are buttons, or these hands can fold
into a clasp, or else these fingers make a zip
or buckle, you say which. Step backwards into it
and try the same canary-yellow cotton jacket, there,
like this, for size again. It still fits.

# The Mariner's Compass

Living alone, I'm sailing the world
single-handed in a rented house.
Last week I rounded the Cape of Good Hope,
came through in one piece;

this morning, flying fish
lying dead in the porch with the post.
I peg out duvet covers and sheets
to save fuel when the wind blows,

tune the engine so it purrs all night
like a fridge, run upstairs
with the old-fashioned thought
of plotting a course by the stars.

Friends wave from the cliffs,
talk nervously from the coastguard station.
Under the rules, close contact
with another soul means disqualification.

*from* KILLING TIME

DISTRIBUTIONS

§

Meanwhile, somewhere in the state of Colorado, armed to the teeth
    with thousands of flowers,
two boys entered the front door of their own high school
    and for almost four hours
gave floral tributes to fellow students and members of staff,
    beginning with red roses
strewn amongst unsuspecting pupils during their lunch hour,
    followed by posies
of peace lilies and wild orchids. Most thought the whole show
    was one elaborate hoax
using silk replicas of the real things, plastic imitations,
    exquisite practical jokes,
but the flowers were no more fake than you or I,
    and were handed out
as compliments returned, favours repaid, in good faith,
    straight from the heart.
No would not be taken for an answer. Therefore a daffodil
    was tucked behind the ear
of a boy in a baseball hat, and marigolds and peonies
    threaded through the hair
of those caught on the stairs or spotted along corridors,
    until every pupil
who looked up from behind a desk could expect to be met
    with at least a petal
or a dusting of pollen, if not an entire daisy-chain,
    or the colour-burst
of a dozen foxgloves, flowering for all their worth,
    or a buttonhole to the breast.
Upstairs in the school library, individuals were singled out
    for special attention:

some were showered with blossom, others wore their blooms
    like brooches or medallions;
even those who turned their backs or refused point-blank
    to accept such honours
were decorated with buds, unseasonable fruits and rosettes
    the same as the others.
By which time a crowd had gathered outside the school,
    drawn through suburbia
by the rumour of flowers in full bloom, drawn through the air
    like butterflies to buddleia,
like honey bees to honeysuckle, like hummingbirds
    dipping their tongues in,
some to soak up such over-exuberance of thought, others
    to savour the goings-on.
Finally, overcome by their own munificence or hay fever,
    the flower-boys pinned
the last blooms on themselves, somewhat selfishly perhaps,
    but had also planned
further surprises for those who swept through the aftermath
    of broom and buttercup:
garlands and bouquets were planted in lockers and cupboards,
    timed to erupt
like the first day of spring into the arms of those
    who, during the first bout,
either by fate or chance had somehow been overlooked
    and missed out.
Experts are now trying to say how two apparently quiet kids
    from an apple-pie town
could get their hands on a veritable rainforest of plants
    and bring down

a whole botanical digest of one species or another onto the heads
 of classmates and teachers,
and where such fascination began, and why it should lead
 to an outpouring of this nature.
And even though many believe that flowers should be kept
 in expert hands
only, or left to specialists in the field such as florists,
 the law of the land
dictates that God, guts and gardening made the country
 what it is today
and for as long as the flower industry can see to it
 things are staying that way.
What they reckon is this: deny a person the right to carry
 flowers of his own
and he's liable to wind up on the business end of a flower
 somebody else has grown.
As for the two boys, it's back to the same old debate:
 is it something in the mind
that grows from birth, like a seed, or is it society
 makes a person that kind?

*from* MISTER HERACLES

## Messenger

It was just happenchance I was present,
the way that a person walking the beach
or harbour might be asked to photograph
a sweet family grouping with their camera,
or the way a person walking the street
might be called in to witness a marriage
by lending himself and his signature.
I was the complete and utter stranger,
invited in as a good-luck gesture,
first footer, bringing in the new era.
The old enemy lay dead in one corner,
killed like the wolf in range of the cradle.
The family closed rank, held hands in the round,
Heracles, his father, wife and three sons,
with their arms crossed over. Purifying water
in a bowl was set down centre-circle.
Heracles moved forward, then seemed to stall,
and a nerve pumped in the wall of his neck,
just here, as if the man couldn't swallow,
and his eyes swelled in their sockets. His veins
were hot, overloaded, and he mumbled,
'Father, this isn't the time to clean the house,
I have breakthroughs to make, barriers to crash,
more dirty work to do before I stop.
No rest for the wicked indeed. No peace.'
Then he sat down on the arm of the chair
as if it were the saddle of a horse
or the captain's seat, and lashed with the reins
and play-acted with levers and controls.
And everyone smiled nervously, not sure

whether to meet his eye with laughter or fear.
And he bucked and galloped and kangarooed
around the room, to and fro, side to side,
still riding his imaginary ride.
The next thing, he threw himself to the ground,
saying the earth was a feast on a plate,
and licked the floor and ate coal from the grate,
then forced his way through a pretend thicket
into a pretend wood, then stripped naked,
then held an arm-wrestling competition
with some invisible opposing force,
then got dressed again claiming to have won.
And his father took his arm and said, 'Son,
what is this journey you travel on?
Give us some clue or sign. Is it the past
that plays on your mind, troubles your mind's eye?'
But Heracles pushed the old man aside
and a rage entered his face, and, help me,
God, to tell what came next. Give me strength to say.
He turned then to his children, not to hold
or lift them or love them, but to kill them.
And the steel in his eyes gave him away,
because one ran to hide in the shadows,
and one rolled underneath a stone table,
and one hid in the skirts of his mother,
and the mother screamed, 'You are their father,
their father, for pity's sake, Heracles . . .'
And chaos broke out all over the house.
And Heracles strode into the shadows
and collared his eldest son by the neck

and brought his free hand sledgehammering down
with such force that the boy's head truly split,
and his mouth poured with blood, and both eyes bled.
'Here's one I'm killing for the mother state,'
he said, throwing the boy down in a dead heap.
Then he walked to where his second son hid
and lifted up the stone table, as if
it were nothing more than a suitcase lid.
The boy jumped up into his father's arms,
hugging him, pleading, begging for his life,
his small voice crying out not to be hurt.
Those cries went unheard. And being too close,
too near at hand for a swing of the fist,
Heracles simply locked his arms and squeezed,
and squeezed, crushing his son's ribs, crushing bones
and breath, until no sound or life was left.
'And here's a killing for the greater good,'
he yelled, and threw the body to one side.
Then seeing the mother and the youngest son
running for their lives, he steadied himself,
reached down towards his belt, and with a gun
emptied the whole barrel into them both,
then put the gun to his father's head
and clicked the trigger, but the last bullet
was spent. His father stared into mid-air,
his face without blood, full of blankness, drained.
Heracles stood for a moment, then swayed
and fell, crashing head-first through a glass pane.
And seeing our chance, we tied him with ropes
and rolled him in chains, and he sleeps now,

the killer of his three sons and his wife,
muscles flickering and flinching with dreams.
So help us all. This is what I have seen.

*from* THE UNIVERSAL HOME DOCTOR

# The Shout

We went out
into the school yard together, me and the boy
whose name and face

I don't remember. We were testing the range
of the human voice:
he had to shout for all he was worth,

I had to raise an arm
from across the divide to signal back
that the sound had carried.

He called from over the park – I lifted an arm.
Out of bounds,
he yelled from the end of the road,

from the foot of the hill,
from beyond the look-out post of Fretwell's Farm –
I lifted an arm.

He vanished from sight, went on to be twenty years dead
with a gunshot hole
in the roof of his mouth, in Western Australia.

Boy with the name and face I don't remember,
you can stop shouting now, I can still hear you.

## All for One

Why is it my mind won't leave me alone?
All day it sits on the arm of the chair
plucking grey hairs like thoughts out of my skull,
flicking my ear with a Duralon comb.

Evenings when I need to work, get things done;
nine o'clock, my mind stands with its coat on
in the hall. Sod it. We drive to the pub,
it drinks, so yours truly has to drive home.

I leave at sunrise in the four-wheel drive –
my mind rides shotgun on the running board,
taps on the window of my log-cabin,
wants to find people and go night-clubbing.

Social call – my mind has to tag along.
Hangs off at first, plays it cool, smiles its smile;
next minute – launches into song. Then what?
Only cops off with the belle of the belle

of the ball – that's all. Main man. Life and soul.
Makes hand-shadows on the living-room wall.
Recites 'Albert and the Lion', in French,
stood on its head drinking a yard of ale.

Next morning over paracetamol and toast
my mind weeps crocodile tears of remorse
onto the tablecloth. *Can't we be close?*
I look my mind square in the face and scream:

mind, find your own family and friends to love;
mind, open your own high-interest account;
offer yourself the exploding cigar;
put whoopee-cushions under your own arse.

It's a joke. I flounce out through the front door;
my mind in its slippers and dressing gown
runs to the garden and catches my sleeve,
says what it's said a hundred times before.

From a distance it must look like a strange sight:
two men of identical shape, at odds
at first, then joined by an outstretched arm, one
leading the other back to his own home.

# Chainsaw versus the Pampas Grass

It seemed an unlikely match. All winter unplugged,
grinding its teeth in a plastic sleeve, the chainsaw swung
nose-down from a hook in the darkroom
under the hatch in the floor. When offered the can
it knocked back a quarter-pint of engine oil
and juices ran from its joints and threads,
oozed across the guide-bar and the maker's name,
into the dry links.

From the summerhouse, still holding one last gulp
of last year's heat behind its double doors, and hung
with the weightless wreckage of wasps and flies,
mothballed in spider's wool . . .
from there, I trailed the day-glo orange power line
the length of the lawn and the garden path,
fed it out like powder from a keg, then walked
back to the socket and flicked the switch, then walked again
and coupled the saw to the flex – clipped them together.
Then dropped the safety catch and gunned the trigger.

No gearing up or getting to speed, just an instant rage,
the rush of metal lashing out at air, connected to the mains.
The chainsaw with its perfect disregard, its mood
to tangle with cloth, or jewellery, or hair.
The chainsaw with its bloody desire, its sweet tooth
for the flesh of the face and the bones underneath,
its grand plan to kick back against nail or knot
and rear up into the brain.

I let it flare, lifted it into the sun
and felt the hundred beats per second drumming in its heart,
and felt the drive-wheel gargle in its throat.

The pampas grass with its ludicrous feathers
and plumes. The pampas grass, taking the warmth and light
from cuttings and bulbs, sunning itself,
stealing the show with its footstools, cushions and tufts
and its twelve-foot spears.
This was the sledgehammer taken to crack the nut.
Probably all that was needed here was a good pull or shove
or a pitchfork to lever it out at its base.
Overkill. I touched the blur of the blade
against the nearmost tip of a reed – it didn't exist.
I dabbed at a stalk that swooned, docked a couple of heads,
dismissed the top third of its canes with a sideways sweep
at shoulder height – this was a game.
I lifted the fringe of undergrowth, carved at the trunk –
plant-juice spat from the pipes and tubes
and dust flew out as I ripped into pockets of dark, secret
    warmth.

To clear a space to work
I raked whatever was severed or felled or torn
towards the dead zone under the outhouse wall, to be fired.
Then cut and raked, cut and raked, till what was left
was a flat stump the size of a barrel lid
that wouldn't be dug with a spade or prised from the earth.
Wanting to finish things off I took up the saw

and drove it vertically downwards into the upper roots,
but the blade became choked with soil or fouled with weeds,
or what was sliced or split somehow closed and mended
   behind,
like cutting at water or air with a knife.
I poured barbecue fluid into the patch
and threw in a match – it flamed for a minute, smoked
for a minute more, and went out. I left it at that.

In the weeks that came new shoots like asparagus tips
sprang up from its nest and by June
it was riding high in its saddle, wearing a new crown.
Corn in Egypt. I looked on
from the upstairs window like the midday moon.

Back below stairs on its hook the chainsaw seethed.
I left it a year, to work back through its man-made dreams,
to try to forget.
The seamless urge to persist was as far as it got.

# The Strid

After tying the knot,
whatever possessed us to make for the Strid?

That crossing point
on the River Wharfe

which famously did
for the boy and his dog;

that tourist trap
where a catchment area comes to a head

in a bottleneck stream
above Bolton Abbey;

you in your dress of double cream,
me done up like a tailor's dummy.

Surely it's more of a lover's leap:
two back-to-back rocks

hydraulically split
by the incompressible sap of the spine;

let it be known
that between two bodies made one

there's more going on
than they'd have us believe.

Whatever possessed us, though?
Was it the pink champagne talking?

Or all for the sake of carrying on,
canoodling out of doors,

the fuck of the century under the stars?
Or the leather-soled shoes

with the man-made uppers,
bought on the never-never,

moulded and stitched
for the purpose of taking us

up and across, over the threshold
of water-cut rock and localised moss

in one giant stride,
bridegroom and bride?

A week goes by,
then the rain delivers:

you, like the death of a swan
in a bed of reeds,

me, like a fish gone wrong
a mile down river;

exhibits X and Y,
matching rings on swollen fingers,

and proof beyond doubt
of married life –

the coroner's voice, proclaiming us
dead to the world, husband and wife.

# The Twang

Well it was St George's Day in New York.
They'd dyed the Hudson with cochineal and chalk.
Bulldogs were arse-to-mouth in Central Park.
Midtown, balloons drifted up, red and white streamers

flowed like plasma and milk. The Mayor on a float on Fifth,
resplendent, sunlight detonating on his pearly suit.
The President followed, doing the Lambeth Walk.
It was an election year on both counts. In the Royal Oak

boiled beef was going for a song. Some Dubliner
played along, came out with cockney rhyming slang,
told jokes against his own and spoke of cousins twice
    removed
from Islington, which made him one of us.

A paper dragon tripped down Lexington, its tongue
truly forked. Two hands thrust from its open throat:
in the left, a red rose; in the right, a collection box
for the National Trust. I mean the National Front.

# The Laughing Stock

October. Post meridian. Seven o'clock. We've had tea.
Chip pans cool on pantry shelves. Now we can lounge
on broken settees, scoff bite-size portions of chocolate and fat,
crack open a tinnie or two. Skin up. Channel hop.

We're keeping an ounce of toot in a tin for a rainy day.
We talk about work – which corners we cut. Our dogs
lick at the plates on the floor, snort at the ashtray.
Our children are bored, they'll go in the army.

The news was the usual stuff. Like a fire
the telly stays on all the time and our faces and hands
are tanned with the glare. Sit-coms are *so* funny.
The nights draw in, like someone left a tap running.

We're watching a show: *How the Other Half Live*.
Apparently, even at this late hour of an evening, couples
are just setting out to eat. They're friends of the Queen,
as likely as not, and peasant cuisine is an absolute must,

with the wine of the month. Cutlery waits in position.
On FM stations, dinner-jazz plays through open curtains.

Arse-time. Weight off the spine. The hour of the couch.
Now and again, one of us scrubs up well, crosses
the border, gets so far then opens his cake-hole,
asks for meals by the wrong name, in the wrong order.

Why bother? The dishes can wait; we're washing our hair
in the sink, soaking our feet in a bowl. Our dogs
are a joke, disgusting, coming to sniff and to drink
like animal things at the watering hole.

# The Straight and Narrow

When the tall and bearded careers advisor
set up his stall and his slide-projector

something clicked. There on the silver screen,
like a photograph of the human soul,

the X-ray plate of the ten-year-old girl
who swallowed a toy. Shadows and shapes,

mercury-tinted lungs and a tin-foil heart,
alloy organs and tubes, but bottom left,

the caught-on-camera lightning strike
of the metal car: like a neon bone,

some classic roadster with an open top
and a man at the wheel in goggles and cap,

motoring on through deep, internal dark.
The clouds opened up; we were leaving the past,

drawn by a star that had risen inside us,
some as astronauts and some as taxi-drivers.

# Birthday

Bed. Sheets without sleep, and the first birds.
Dawn at the pace of a yacht.

The first bus, empty, carries its cargo of light
from the depot, like a block of ice.

Dawn when the mind looks out of its nest,
dawn with gold in its teeth.

In the street, a milk-float moves
by throw of a dice,

the mast to the east raises itself
to its full height. Elsewhere

someone's husband touches someone's wife.
One day older the planet weeps.

This is the room
where I found you one night,

bent double, poring over
the *Universal Home Doctor,*

that bible of death, atlas of ill-health:
hand-drawn, colour-coded diagrams of pain,

*chromosomal abnormalities* explained,
*progesterone secretion,*

*cervical incompetence . . .*
Susan, for God's sake.

I had to edge towards it,
close the cover with my bare foot.

Dawn when the mind looks out of its nest.
Dawn with gold in its teeth.

From the window I watch
Anubis, upright in black gloves

making a sweep of the earth
under the nameless tree,

pushing through shrubs,
checking the bin for bones or meat

then leaving with a backward glance, in his own time,
crossing the lawn and closing the gate.

# The Summerhouse

With the right tools it was less than a day's work.
It wasn't our trade, but a wire-brush was the thing
for fettling mould and moss from bevelled window frames.
Sandpaper took back old wood to its true grain.

Winter pressed its handshake, even through thick gloves.
From the boozy warmth of the boiler-room I lugged
a litre tin of Weatherseal, and popped the lid.
Strange brew. Varnish or paint? Water-based, it had a tone

or shade, but carried solvent on its breath
and held the stars and planets of a pinhole universe
suspended in its depth. Some gemstone in its liquid state –
it fumed when ruffled with a garden cane.

Winter stood on the toe-end of leather boots.
And as the substance in the tin went down it lost its shine,
and from its lower reaches came a sluggishness –
a thick, begrudging treacle, and the colour brown.

Some change in temperature was the root cause.
Rifles stamped their feet and clapped their hands together
over on the firing-range. It was going dark
but unconcerned we dipped the brushes for a second coat.

It was time-travel, of a sort. Having given our all
to this chapel of sunloungers and soft drinks,
to the obvious glory of ultraviolet light, we found ourselves
standing instead by a wooden shed, painted with mud and shit.

# The Back Man

Five strong, we were, not including the guide,
five of us walking a well-trodden path
through the reserve, from the camp to the stream
and the flooded forest on the far side.
Dragonflies motored past like fish on the wing.
Beetles lifted their solar-panelled shells.
A bird, invisible, ran through its scale
like a thumbnail strummed on a metal comb.
The branches of trees were shelves in a shop
selling insect brooches and snakeskin belts
and miniature frogs with enamelled heads.
The monkeys fancied themselves as soft toys.
Blue orchids offered themselves without shame.
Late afternoon, and the heat in the shade
was stale and gross, a queasy, airless warmth,
centuries old. I was the last in line,

the back man, when from out of nowhere
it broke, I mean flew at me from behind,
and I saw in my mind's eye the carved mask
of its face, the famous robe of black fur,
the pins and amulets of claws and feet,
the crown and necklace of its jaws and teeth
all spearing into the nape of my neck.
I dropped the hunting knife and the shooting stick.

The rest of the group had moved on ahead.
The blades and feathers of grasses and ferns
conducted something in the air, but time
was static, jammed shut. Nerves strained with the sense

of a trap half-sprung, a pin almost pulled
and all noise was a tight thread stretched and thinned
to breaking point, and blood in its circuit
awaited a pulse. The turnpike of a branch
bent slowly back to shape across the trail.
Up high, a treetop craned its weathervane;
a storm-cloud split and it started to rain.
I was shouldered home in the fibreglass tomb
of a yellow canoe. Then sat up straight –
alive. Unharmed, in fact. In fact untouched.

I've heard it said that a human face
shaved in the hairs on the back of a head
can stop a jaguar dead in its tracks,
the way a tattoo of Christ, crucified
across the shoulder blades and down the spine,
in past times, could save a thief from the lash.
Years on, nothing has changed. I'm still the man
to be hauled down, ripped apart, but a sharp
backward glance, as it were, is all it takes.
I sense it mostly in the day-to-day:
not handling some rare gem or art object
but flicking hot fat over a bubbling egg,
test-flying a stunt-kite from Blackstone Edge,
not swearing to tell the whole truth on oath
but bending to read the meter with a torch,
tonguing the seamless flux of a gold tooth,
not shaking the hands of serial killers
but dead-heading dogwood with secateurs,
eyeballing blue tits through binoculars,

not crossing the great ocean by pedalo
but moseying forward in the middle lane,
hanging wallpaper flush to the plumb-line,
not barrelling over sky-high waterfalls
but brass-rubbing the hallmarks of fob-watches,
lying on top of sex, in the afterwards,
not metal-detecting the beach for land-mines
but tilting the fins of pinball machines,
pencilling snidey comments in the margins,
not escaping into freedom or peacetime
but trousering readies extruded from cashpoints,
eating the thick air that blasts the escarpment,
not rising to the bait of a fur coat
but yacking on the cordless, cruising Ceefax,
checking the pollen count and long-range forecast,
not whipping up the mother-of-all soufflés
but picking off clay pipes with an air rifle
at the side-show, describing myself as
white in the tick-box, dipping the dipstick,
needling pips from half a pomegranate,
not cranking up the system to overload
but licking the Christian Aid envelope,
lining up a family photograph,
not chasing twisters across Oklahoma
but changing a flat tyre on the hard shoulder,
dowsing for Channel 4 with a coat hanger,
not carving a slice from the Golden Calf
but hiking the town's municipal golf course,
drowning an inner tube in a horse trough,
not feeling the sonic boom bodily

but swiping a key card in the hotel lobby,
easing up for the lollipop lady,
not inhabiting the divine sepulchre,
not crowing over Arctic adventure,
not standing gob-smacked beneath ancient sculpture,
not kneeling empty-handed, open-mouthed
at the altar, but in the barber's chair
or tattoo parlour, in a sleepy trance,
catching in the mirror the startled face
of some scissor-hand, some needle-finger.

*from* TRAVELLING SONGS

# Killing Time #2

Time in the brain cells sweating like a nail bomb,
trouble with the heartbeat spitting like a Sten gun,
    cut to the chase,
    pick up the pace;
no such thing as a walkabout fun-run,
    shoot yourself a glance in the chrome in the day-room,
don't hang about, you're running out of space, son.

Red light, stop sign, belly full of road rage,
ticket from the fuzz if you dawdle in the slow lane,
    pull up your socks,
    get out of the blocks;
twelve-hour day-shift grafting at the coal face,
    turning up the gas brings blood to the boat race,
strike with the iron or you're sleeping in the Stone Age.

Don't dilly-dally or the trail goes cold, sir,
don't hold back till you're mouldy old dough, sir,
    sprint for the line,
    turn on a dime;
sit tight, hang fire, I'm putting you on hold, sir,
    too late, snail pace, already sold, sir,
blame it on the kids but it's you getting old, sir.

Short cut, fast track, trolley dash at Kwik Save,
four-minute warning, boil yourself an egg, babe,
    crack the whip,
    shoot from the hip;
close shave, tear arse, riding on a knife blade,
    twenny-four-seven in the brain-drain rat race,
finger on the pulse but you'd better watch your heart rate.

Cheap thrills, speed kills, pop yourself a pill, mate,
thumb a free ride on amphetamine sulphate,
  run with the pack,
  don't look back;
pedal to the floor when you're burning up the home straight,
  her indoors doesn't want you getting home late,
love's in the freezer and your dinner's in the dog-grate.

Ten to the dozen to the grave from the carry-cot,
bolt like a thoroughbred, talk like a chatterbox,
  oil the wheels,
  pick up your heels;
ginseng tea turns out to be tommyrot,
  reach for the future with a hand full of liver-spots,
fuse-wire burns in the barrel of a body-clock.

Cut yourself in half doing life at the sharp end,
meet your own self coming back around the U-bend,
  get with the beat,
  turn up the heat;
sink like a stone by going off the deep end,
  fifty quid an hour for a top-flight shrink, said
start killing time, it's later than you think, friend.

★

I've started to think
about life on the drink
and I'm sailing out into the blue.
And there's room in the cabin for two.
So float like a cork and then put into port for me,
crew for me, stew for me, boil up a brew for me,
all the way over the sea.

I'm right on the brink
of life on the drink
and I'm sailing out into the blue.
And there's room in the cabin for two.
So stay for me, pray for me, cough up and pay for me,
sob for me, slob for me, break out the grog for me,
jibe for me, tack for me, take up the slack for me,
slurp for me, burp for me, load up a crate for me,
turpentine's great for me,
work up a thirst for me,
put yourself first for me,
bob for me, toss for me, climb on your cross for me,
all the way over the sea.

I've started to sink
into life on the drink
and I'm sailing out into the blue.
And there's room in the cabin for two.
So duck for me, dive for me, bum me a five for me,
dress for me, stress for me, wipe up the mess for me,
pass up the rest for me,
stick out your chest for me,

[133]

boke for me, choke for me, crack me a joke for me,
light up a smoke for me,
get out and graft for me,
rig up a raft for me,
nip for me, tuck for me, ride out your luck for me,
vouch for me, crouch for me, open your pouch for me,
lather me, razor me, Mother Teresa me,
don't ask me why for me,
live me a lie for me,
bleed yourself dry and then sod off and die for me,
all the way over the sea.

# Going Up

Lived in a boot.
Hand-made calf-skin, fitted dead snug.
Rolled down tongue so it was open-top.
Jehovah's Witnesses didn't know where to knock.
Not 100% waterproof but good enough.
Drank beer over garden wall of ankle cuff.
Lived in a boot.

Lived in a boot.
Peered through eyelets
like a sailor coming into port.
Picnicked outside on toe-end like it was Castle Hill.
Salt mark – like tide mark around bath – wouldn't come off.
No fucker visited, but so what?
Lived in a boot.

Lived in a boot.
Pulled laces tight on nights with no moon.
Kept loaded twelve-bore in hollowed-out heel.
More and more neighbours in slip-ons and brogues.
Less and less walks, stayed home to keep guard.
Lived in a boot.

Lived in a boot.
Wore down on one side – started to rock.
Scuff marks and cracks, polish and dubbin – couldn't be
    faffed.

Toxocariasis from shit from dogs – owners should be shot.
Leather went saggy like an old face, nails came through.
Stitching rotted around welt, insoles went manky,
smelt.

Didn't do any more, didn't suit.
Moved out. Moved to a hat.

## Leaves on the Line

In the past he was coming by steam and coal,
by breath of water, flame of stone;
we waited for hours then buggered off home.

> Till Leaf Man come
> how long, how long?

At present he comes by diesel or spark;
with an ear to the rail we can hear him talk.
We wait all day then die in the dark.

> How sung, how sung
> the Leaf Man song?

Tomorrow he'll come on a beam of light,
rise like morning, end this wait,
but the rooster croaked and he's already late.

> Till Leaf Man come, how long, how long,
> how sung, how sung the Leaf Man song?

*from* TYRANNOSAURUS REX
VERSUS THE CORDUROY KID

# On Marsden Moor

Above the tree line and below the fog
I watched two men on the opposite slope
hauling wooden poles and slabs of dressed stone
from the foot of the hill towards the top.

They didn't stall – just lifted, carried, dropped.
I watched for an hour or thereabouts,
way off, but close enough in a straight line
to bundle them over with a big shout.

Away from the five o'clock of the town,
out from under the axles and bruised skies
it bothered me that men should hike this far
to hoick timber and rock up a steep bank.

Because what if those poles were fencing posts
to hammer home, divide a plot of land
between the two of them, and those dumb stones
the first steps to a new Jerusalem?

# Horses, M62

Sprung from a field,
a team
of a dozen or so

is suddenly here and amongst,
silhouettes
in the butterscotch dusk.

One ghosts
between vans,
traverses three lanes,

its chess-piece head
fording the river of fumes;
one jumps the barricades

between carriageways;
a third slows
to a halt

then bends, nosing
the road, tonguing the surface
for salt.

Standstill.
Motor oil pulses.
Black blood.

Some trucker
swings down from his cab
to muster and drove; but

unbiddable, crossbred nags
they scatter
through ginnels

of coachwork and chrome,
and are distant, gone,
then a dunch

and here alongside
is a horse,
the writhing mat of its hide

pressed on the glass –
a tank of worms –
a flank

of actual horse . . .
It bolts,
all arse and tail

through a valley
of fleet saloons.
Regrouped they clatter away,

then spooked by a horn
double back,
a riderless charge,

a flack of horseshoe and hoof
into the idling cars,
now eyeball, nostril, tooth

under the sodium glow,
biblical, eastbound,
against the flow.

# A Vision

The future was a beautiful place, once.
Remember the full-blown balsa-wood town
on public display in the Civic Hall?
The ring-bound sketches, artists' impressions,

blueprints of smoked glass and tubular steel,
board-game suburbs, modes of transportation
like fairground rides or executive toys.
Cities like *dreams*, cantilevered by light.

And people like us at the bottle bank
next to the cycle path, or dog-walking
over tended strips of fuzzy-felt grass,
or model drivers, motoring home in

electric cars. Or after the late show –
strolling the boulevard. They were the plans,
all underwritten in the neat left-hand
of architects – a true, legible script.

I pulled that future out of the north wind
at the landfill site, stamped with today's date,
riding the air with other such futures,
all unlived in and now fully extinct.

# Causeway

Three walked barefoot into the sea,
mother, father and only child
with trousers rolled above the knee.
A stretch of water – half a mile;
granite loaves made a cobbled road
when the tide was low. Tide was high.
Bread vans idled on either shore.
In lifeboat sheds along the coast
cradled boats were dead to the world –
the bones of reassembled whales.
A mothballed helicopter dozed.
But three unshod went wading on,
father, mother and little one,
up to their hips in brine and krill,
the Gulf Stream nudging at their heels,
husband, wife and three-year-old,
out of their depth and further still,
over their heads in surf and swell,
further, further, under then gone.
The lifeguard yawned a megaphone.
The oyster-catcher clenched its fist.
The common dolphin bit its lip.
The paraglider pulled away.
The scuba diver held his breath.
Then three appeared. Two heads at first
and then the third, now figurines
emergent, shoeless, plodding on
towards the slipway and the quay.
Three forms. They stopped and turned and faced.
So hundreds followed in their wake,

some on Zimmer frames, some on stilts,
some in wellies and some on bikes,
one with gravy stains up his tie;
thousands legging it down the beach,
some in khaki and some in kilts,
some in purdah and fancy dress,
one with a monkey round his neck.
And more. In fact the bastard lot.
(Two rivers, west and east, now burst
with caribou and wildebeest.)
And woman, man and only child,
the three with trousers rolled who strolled
across the bay, were cast in bronze –
barefoot, blameless, set to stand
above the millions who drowned.

## You're Beautiful

because you're classically trained.
I'm ugly because I associate piano wire with strangulation.

You're beautiful because you stop to read the cards in
    newsagents' windows about lost cats and missing dogs.
I'm ugly because of what I did to that jellyfish with a lolly
    stick and a big stone.

You're beautiful because for you, politeness is instinctive, not
    a marketing campaign.
I'm ugly because desperation is impossible to hide.

> *Ugly like he is,*
> *Beautiful like hers,*
> *Beautiful like Venus,*
> *Ugly like his,*
> *Beautiful like she is,*
> *Ugly like Mars.*

You're beautiful because you believe in coincidence and the
    power of thought.
I'm ugly because I proved God to be a mathematical
    improbability.

You're beautiful because you prefer home-made soup to the
    packet stuff.
I'm ugly because once, at a dinner party, I defended the
    aristocracy and wasn't even drunk.

You're beautiful because you can't work the remote control.
I'm ugly because of satellite television and twenty-four-hour
    rolling news.

> *Ugly like he is,*
> *Beautiful like hers,*
> *Beautiful like Venus,*
> *Ugly like his,*
> *Beautiful like she is,*
> *Ugly like Mars.*

You're beautiful because you cry at weddings as well as
    funerals.
I'm ugly because I think of children as another species from
    a different world.

You're beautiful because you look great in any colour
    including red.
I'm ugly because I think shopping is strictly for the
    acquisition of material goods.

You're beautiful because when you were born, undiscovered
    planets lined up to peep over the rim of your cradle and lay
    gifts of gravity and light at your miniature feet.
I'm ugly for saying 'love at first sight' is another form of
    mistaken identity, and that the most human of all responses
    is to gloat.

*Ugly like he is,*
*Beautiful like hers,*
*Beautiful like Venus,*
*Ugly like his,*
*Beautiful like she is,*
*Ugly like Mars.*


You're beautiful because you've never seen the inside of a
   car-wash.
I'm ugly because I always ask for a receipt.

You're beautiful for sending a box of shoes to the third world.
I'm ugly because I remember the telephone numbers of
   ex-girlfriends and the year Schubert was born.

You're beautiful because you sponsored a parrot in a zoo.
I'm ugly because when I sigh it's like the slow collapse of a
   circus tent.

You're beautiful because you can point at a man in a uniform
   and laugh.
I'm ugly because I was a police informer in a previous life.

You're beautiful because you drink a litre of water and eat
   five pieces of fruit a day.
I'm ugly for taking the line that a meal without meat is a
   beautiful woman with one eye.

You're beautiful because you don't see love as a competition
    and you know how to lose.
I'm ugly because I kissed the FA Cup then held it up to the
    crowd.

You're beautiful because of a single buttercup in the top
    buttonhole of your cardigan.
I'm ugly because I said the World's Strongest Woman was a
    muscleman in a dress.

You're beautiful because you couldn't live in a lighthouse.
I'm ugly for making hand-shadows in front of the giant lamp,
    so when they look up, the captains of vessels in distress see
    the ears of a rabbit, or the eye of a fox, or the legs of a
    galloping black horse.

> *Ugly like he is,*
> *Beautiful like hers,*
> *Beautiful like Venus,*
> *Ugly like his,*
> *Beautiful like she is,*
> *Ugly like Mars.*

> *Ugly like he is,*
> *Beautiful like hers,*
> *Beautiful like Venus,*
> *Ugly like his,*
> *Beautiful like she is,*
> *Ugly like Mars.*

## To the Women of the Merrie England
## Coffee Houses, Huddersfield

O women of the Merrie England Coffee Houses, Huddersfield,
when I break sweat just thinking about hard work, I think
    about you.
Nowhere to hide behind that counter, nowhere to shirk.
I'm watching you right now bumping and grinding hip to hip,
I'm noting your scrubbed pink hands in the cabinet of fancy
    cakes,
loose and quick among the lemon meringues and cream puffs
and custard tarts, darting and brushing like carp in a glass
    tank.

O women, the soles of your feet on fire in your sensible shoes,
your fingers aflame, spitting and hissing under the grill.
You, madam, by the cauldron of soup – you didn't hassle us,
just wiped the crumbs from under our genius poems,
me and the boy Smith, one toasted teacake between us,
eking it out through the dead afternoons, our early drafts
hallmarked and franked with rings of coffee and tea.

Women of the Merrie England, under those scarlet aprons are
    you naked?
Are you calendar girls? Miss July traps a swarm of steam in
    a jug
as perspiration rolls from the upper delta of her open neck
to where Christ crucified bobs and twists on a gold chain.
Miss April delivers the kiss of life to a Silk Cut by the fire
    escape.
Miss November, pass me the key to the toilets, please,
I won't violate your paintwork, desecrate the back of the door

with crude anatomical shapes or the names of speedway stars.
I'm no closet queen in search of a glory hole for gay sex,
no smackhead needing a cubbyhole to shoot up –
one glass of your phosphorescing, radioactive orange crush
was always enough for me and the boy Smith, his mother
asleep at the wheel on the long drive back from Wales,
the airbag not invented yet – just a bubble in somebody's dream.

Does he pay you a pittance in groats, King Henry, stuffing his
    face
with hare and swan, his beard dyed red with venison blood
and pinned with the fiddling bones of partridge and quail,
while you, O women of the Merrie England, his maids,
swab the greasy tiles with a bucket of rain and a bald mop
or check for counterfeit tenners under the sun-tanning light?
A tenner! – still two hours' graft at the minimum wage.

Don't let catering margarine ease off your eternity rings.
Don't lose your marriages down the waste-disposal pipe.
Hang on to your husbands and friends – no sugar daddies
    or lovers
or cafetières for you, O women of the Merrie England,
no camomile or Earl Grey, just take-it-or-leave-it ground or char
served in the time-bitten cups my grandmother sipped from,
hooking the milky membrane aside with a spoon, watching it
    reform.

I've seen you nudging and winking. Look who just dropped
    in, you say,
The Man Who Fell to Earth, wanting tea for one and the
    soup of the day.

I take the window seat and gawp at the steeplejacks: all gone –
Kaye's, the Coach House, Leeds Road, the White Lion and
the Yards.
But you, under the mock Tudor beams, under the fake shields,
under the falsified coats of arms, you go on, you go on
O women of the Merrie England, O mothers of Huddersfield,
O ladies!

# The Clown Punk

Driving home through the shonky side of town,
three times out of ten you'll see the town clown,
like a basket of washing that got up
and walked, towing a dog on a rope. But

don't laugh: every pixel of that man's skin
is shot through with indelible ink;
as he steps out at the traffic lights,
think what he'll look like in thirty years' time –

the deflated face and shrunken scalp
still daubed with the sad tattoos of high punk.
You kids in the back seat who wince and scream
when he slathers his daft mush on the windscreen,

remember the clown punk with his dyed brain,
then picture windscreen wipers, and let it rain.

# Evening

You're twelve. Thirteen at most.
You're leaving the house by the back door.
There's still time. You've promised
not to be long, not to go far.

One day you'll learn the names of the trees.
You fork left under the ridge,
pick up the bridleway between two streams.
Here is Wool Clough. Here is Royd Edge.

The peak still lit by sun. But
evening. Evening overtakes you up the slope.
Dusk walks its fingers up the knuckles of your spine.
Turn on your heel. Back home

your child sleeps in her bed, too big for a cot.
Your wife makes and mends under the light.
You're sorry. You thought
it was early. How did it get so late?

# Roadshow

We were drawn uphill by the noise and light:
a silver, extraterrestrial glow
beyond the hill's head; a deep, cardiovascular
bass in the hill's hollow chest.

We were heavy and slow, each footstep checked
by the pendulum of our unborn child –
a counterweight swinging from Susan's heart.

Day-glo arrows nailed to fences and trees
pointed the way, first along sea-view streets,
past windows dressed with mail-order driftwood
and No Vacancies signs, then a sharp right
through a housing estate where locals emerged
from hedges and gates, pushing tabs and wraps.
Nothing for us.
              So the road levels out.
But the moment we set foot in the park
the lights are cut and the music fades. And

by pure chance, it's precisely at this point
that the universe – having expanded since birth –
reaches its limit and starts to contract.

The crowd dopples past. The crowd pushes on
to nightclubs and fire-holes down in the bay,
inexhaustibly young and countless strong,
streaming away, always streaming away.

# Sloth

As chance would have it, one has come to rest
in the attic room, right over my desk.
Upside down, he hangs from the curtain pole
like a shot beast carried home from the hunt,

but light burns in his eyes; he isn't dead.
A contemplative soul, much like I am,
he's thinking things through, atom by atom,
and hasn't touched the dried fruit and mixed nuts

I left on a plate on the windowsill,
although a mountain range of Toblerone
is thus far unaccounted for. My wife,
the three-times Olympian pentathlete,

wants to trigger his brains with smelling salts,
clip jump-leads on to the lobes of his ears,
*stick a bomb up his arse*. But I'm not sure:
to me the creature looks dazzled or dazed,

like the Big Bang threw him out of his bed,
like evolution took him by surprise.
Those eyes . . . He can stay another week,
till the weather turns. But now back to work:

look, a giant tortoise goes past in a blur.

# The Spelling

I left a spelling at my father's house
written in small coins on his front step.
It said which star I was heading for next,
which channel to watch, which button to press.
I should have waited, given that spelling
a voice, but I was handsome and late.

While I was gone he replied with pebbles
and leaves at my gate. But a storm got up
from the west, sluicing all meaning and shape.

I keep his broken spelling in a tin,
tip it out on the cellar floor, hoping
a letter or even a word might form.
And I am all grief, staring through black space
to meet his eyes, trying to read his face.

*from* HOMER'S ODYSSEY

Then all the men came and added their weight,
hammered that burning stake into his head,
and when the eyeball burst we were soaked in ink,
and the lens crunched and cracked like splintering ice,
and the lashes and eyebrows flared like burning grass,
and we leaned, and heaved, and forced it further in
until the retina sheared, and the optic nerve
spat and seared and spasmed and fused in the heat.
All the while he screamed into the cave,
roared his pain into the booming, echoing rock,
so loud that other one-eyed monsters on the island
came to listen. They gathered outside, more curious
than concerned, and called, 'Hey, you in there,
what's all the fuss and palaver? Who's giving you grief?'
And Cyclops, writhing in pain, his head in flames,
shouted, 'Nobody. Nobody hurts Cyclops. Nobody.'

So they shrugged their shoulders and padded off home.
A master stroke on my part, and it worked.
When we drew out the stake it was like a bung,
like a cork, like a plug – blood spurted and plumed,
but I didn't finish him off, the thick-headed brute. Why?
He'd rolled a stone across the cave's mouth, blocking the gap,
a stone so vast that he alone could shift it from the hole.
And this was the whole point of my ingenious plan.
The flock were cowering away from the noise and flame.
Twines and twisted willow-strands littered the floor.
Each man lashed himself tight under a fat ram,
and two other rams were tethered alongside
to shield him at the flanks as he dangled and clung on.
Then they ambled forward, tottered over the stone floor,
bleated to be let out of the cave for water and pasture,

and Cyclops, even with a smoking hole instead of an eye,
was still a shepherd at heart, so he rolled away the rock,
opened the mouth of the cave and counted them out,
stroking their backs as they wandered into the light:
'Mether, Tether, Mimph, Hither, Lither, Anver, Danver . . .'
The ignorant swine, he released them one at a time,
each big ram with one of my men slung under its gut.
And I was the last man to escape, suspended beneath
the cockiest ram of the lot, my fingers twisted
into the deep shag of his coat, my feet stirrupped
in the swags of elastic skin to the inside of his leg.

Once on the boats with the men and the flock
and the buckets of cheese and barrels of milk,
I goaded Cyclops with taunts, and he hurled rocks
from the cliff but they only caused ripples
that pushed us further to sea. The wide open sea.

And the men cheered and laughed until light . . .
when it dawned on us that nothing had changed.

Still lost, still famished-hearted, still years from home,
but now with Poseidon fuming and writhing below us,
plotting revenge for blinding his one-eyed son.

That act was to haunt us. From then on
we were marked men, locked on a collision course
with the God of the Sea. He lurked in the depths,
a constant presence. We sensed him under the waves.
The boat shivered when he stirred. And if we'd known

the chain of events we'd set in place, the cruelty
and agony that stretched ahead, year after year,
the horror and terror and sadness and loss still to come –
    who knows,
perhaps we'd have chosen to die right there, in the black cave,
out of sight of heaven and without sound.

With our fate now in the hands of the Gods
we drifted on wind and current, hoping again,
hoping against hope, praying, looking for land.

*from* SIR GAWAIN AND THE GREEN KNIGHT

The drawbridge was dropped, and the double-fronted gates
were unbarred and each half was heaved wide open.
As he clears the planking he crosses himself quickly,
and praises the porter, who kneels before the prince
and prays that God be good to Gawain.
Then he went on his way with the one whose task
was to point out the road to that perilous place
where the knight would receive the slaughterman's strike.
They scrambled up bankings where branches were bare,
clambered up cliff-faces crazed by the cold.
The clouds which had climbed now cooled and dropped
so the moors and the mountains were muzzy with mist
and every hill wore a hat of mizzle on its head.
The streams on the slopes seemed to fume and foam,
whitening the wayside with spume and spray.
They wandered onwards through the wildest woods
till the sun, at that season, came skyward, showing
                    its hand.
            On hilly heights they ride,
            snow littering the land.
            The servant at his side
            then has them slow and stand.

'I have accompanied you across this countryside, my lord,
and now we are nearing the site you have named
and have steered and searched for with such singleness of mind.
But there's something I should like to share with you, sir,
because upon my life, you're a lord that I love,
so if you value your health you'll hear my advice:
the place you head for holds a hidden peril.

[169]

In that wilderness lives a wildman, the worst in the world,
he is brooding and brutal and loves bludgeoning humans.
He's more powerful than any person alive on this planet
and four times the figure of any fighting knight
in King Arthur's castle, Hector included.
And it's at the green chapel where this grisliness goes on,
and to pass through that place unscathed is impossible,
for he deals out death blows by dint of his hands,
a man without measure who shows no mercy.
Be it chaplain or churl who rides by his church,
monk or priest, whatever man or person,
he loves murdering more than he loves his own life.
So I say, just as sure as you sit in your saddle,
to find him is fatal, Gawain – that's a fact.
Trust me, he could trample you twenty times over
                    or more.
          He's lurked about too long
          engaged in grief and gore.
          His hits are swift and strong –
          he'll fell you to the floor.

'So banish that bogeyman to the back of your mind,
and for God's sake travel an alternative track,
ride another road, and be rescued by Christ.
I'll head off home, and with hand on heart
I shall swear by God and all his good saints,
and on all earthly holiness, and other such oaths,
that your secret is safe, and not a soul will know
that you fled in fear from the fellow I described.'
'Many thanks,' said Gawain, in a terse tone of voice,

'and for having my interests at heart, be lucky.
I'm certain such a secret would be silent in your keep.
But as faithful as you are, if I failed to find him
and lost my mettle in the manner you mentioned,
I'd be christened a coward, and could not be excused.
So I'll trek to the chapel and take my chances,
have it out with that ogre, speak openly to him,
whether fairness or foulness follows, however fate
                        behaves.
            He may be stout and stern
            and standing armed with stave,
            but those who strive to serve
            our Lord, our Lord will save.'


'By Mary,' said the servant, 'you seem to be saying
you're hell-bent on heaping harm on yourself
and losing your life, so I'll delay you no longer.
Set your helmet on your head and your lance in your hand
and ride a route through that rocky ravine
till you're brought to the bottom of that foreboding valley,
then look towards a glade a little to the left
and you'll see in the clearing the site itself,
and the hulking superhuman who inhabits the place.
Now God bless and goodbye, brave Sir Gawain;
for all the wealth in the world I wouldn't walk with you
or go further in this forest by a single footstep.'
With a wrench on the reins he reeled around
and heel-kicked the horse as hard as he could,
and was gone from Gawain, galloping hard
                        for home.

'By Christ, I will not cry,'
announced the knight, 'or groan.
But find good fortune by
the grace of God alone.'

Then he presses ahead, picks up a path,
enters a steep-sided grove on his steed
then goes by and by to the bottom of a gorge
where he wonders and watches – it looks a wild place:
no sign of a settlement anywhere to be seen
but heady heights to both halves of the valley
and set with sabre-toothed stones of such sharpness
no cloud in the sky could escape unscratched.
He stalls and halts, holds the horse still,
glances side to side to glimpse the green chapel
but sees no such thing, which he thinks is strange,
except at mid-distance what might be a mound,
a sort of bald knoll on the bank of a brook
where fell-water surged with frenzied force,
bursting with bubbles as if it had boiled.
He heels the horse, heads for that mound,
grounds himself gracefully and tethers Gringolet,
looping the reins to the limb of a lime.
Then he strides forward and circles the feature,
baffled as to what that bizarre hill could be:
it had a hole at one end and at either side,
and its walls, matted with weeds and moss,
enclosed a cavity, like a kind of old cave

or crevice in the crag – it was all too unclear to
       declare.
    'Green church?' chunters the knight.
    'More like the devil's lair
    where, at the nub of night,
    he makes his morning prayer.'

'For certain,' he says, 'this is a soulless spot,
a ghostly cathedral overgrown with grass,
the kind of kirk where that camouflaged man
might deal in devilment and all things dark.
My five senses inform me that Satan himself
has tricked me in this tryst, intending to destroy me.
This is a haunted house – may it go to hell.
I never came across a church so cursed.'
With head helmeted and lance in hand
he scrambled to the skylight of that strange abyss.
Then he heard on the hillside, from behind a hard rock
and beyond the brook, a blood-chilling noise.
What! It cannoned through the cliffs as if they might crack,
like the scream of a scythe being ground on a stone.
What! It whined and wailed, like a waterwheel.
What! It rasped and rang, raw on the ear.
'My God,' cried Gawain, 'that grinding is a greeting.
My arrival is honoured with the honing of an axe
       up there.
    Then let the Lord decide.
    "Oh well" won't help me here.
    I might well lose my life
    but freak sounds hold no fear.'

Then Gawain called as loudly as his lungs would allow,
'Who has power in this place to honour his pact?
Because good Gawain now walks on this ground.
Whoever will meet him should emerge this moment
and he needs to be fast – it's now or it's never.'
'Abide', came a voice from above the bank.
'You'll cop what's coming to you quickly enough.'
Yet he went at his work, whetting the blade,
not showing until it was sharpened and stropped.
Then out of the crags he comes through the cave-mouth,
whirling into view with a wondrous weapon,
a Danish-style axe for doling out death,
with a brute of a blade curving back to the haft
filed on a stone, a four-footer at least
by the look of the length of its shining lace.
And again he was green, like a year ago,
with green hair and flesh and a fully green face,
and firmly on green feet he came stomping forward,
the handle of that axe like a staff in his hand.
At the edge of the water he will not wade
but vaults the stream with the shaft, and strides
with an ominous face onto earth covered over
                    with snow.
          Our brave knight bowed, his head
          hung low – but not too low!
          'Young sir,' the green man said,
          'your visit keeps your vow.'


The green knight spoke again, 'God guard you, Gawain.
Welcome to my world after all your wandering.

You have timed your arrival like a true traveller
to begin this business which binds us together.
Last year, at this time, what was yielded became yours,
and with New Year come you are called to account.
We're very much alone, beyond view in this valley,
no person to part us – we can do as we please.
Pull your helmet from your head and take what you're owed.
Show no more struggle than I showed myself
when you severed my spine with a single smite.'
'No,' said good Gawain, 'by my life-giving God,
I won't gripe or begrudge the grimness to come,
so keep to one stroke and I'll stand stock still,
won't whisper a word of unwillingness, or one
                    complaint.'
                He bowed to take the blade
                and bared his neck and nape,
                but, loath to look afraid,
                he feigned a fearless state.

Suddenly the green knight summons up his strength,
hoists the axe high over Gawain's head,
lifts it aloft with every fibre of his life
and begins to bring home a bone-splitting blow.
Had he seen it through as thoroughly as threatened
the man beneath him would have met with his maker.
But glimpsing the axe at the edge of his eye
bringing death earthwards as it arced through the air,
and sensing its sharpness, Gawain shrank at the shoulders.
The swinging axe-man swerved from his stroke,
and reproached the young prince with piercing words:

'Call yourself good Sir Gawain?' he goaded.
'Who faced down every foe in the field of battle
but now flinches with fear at the foretaste of harm?
Never have I known such a namby-pamby knight.
Did I budge or even blink when you aimed the axe,
or carp or quibble in King Arthur's castle,
or flap when my head went flying to my feet?
But entirely untouched, you are terror-struck.
I'll be found the better fellow, since you were so feeble
                              and frail.'
                    Gawain confessed, 'I flinched
                    at first, but will not fail.
                    Though once my head's unhitched
                    it's off once and for all!'

*from* OUT OF THE BLUE

You have picked me out.
Through a distant shot of a building burning
you have noticed now
that a white cotton shirt is twirling, turning.

In fact I am waving, waving.
Small in the clouds, but waving, waving.
Does anyone see
a soul worth saving?

So when will you come?
Do you think you are watching, watching
a man shaking crumbs
or pegging out washing?

I am trying and trying.
The heat behind me is bullying, driving,
but the white of surrender is not yet flying.
I am not at the point of leaving, diving.

A bird goes by.
The depth is appalling. Appalling
that others like me
should be wind-milling, wheeling, spiralling, falling.

Are your eyes believing,
believing
that here in the gills
I am still breathing?

But tiring, tiring.
Sirens below are wailing, firing.
My arm is numb and my nerves are sagging.
Do you see me, my love? I am failing, flagging.

*from* THE NOT DEAD

# The Parting Shot

So five graves, like long evening shadows, are dug,
and the five coffins wait in line, varnished and squared off,
and the firing party aims for the distance and fires,
and all are starched and suited and booted and buttoned up.

Then ramrod straight, under the shade of a tree,
the boy-bugler raises a golden horn to his lips,
and calls to his dead friends with his living breath.
And the tune never wavers or breaks,
but now tears roll from his eyes,
tears which fall from his face and bloom
on his ironed green shirt like two dark wounds.

Then the world swims and drowns in everyone else's eyes too.

# The Manhunt

After the first phase,
after passionate nights and intimate days,

only then would he let me trace
the frozen river which ran through his face,

only then would he let me explore
the blown hinge of his lower jaw,

and handle and hold
the damaged, porcelain collarbone,

and mind and attend
the fractured rudder of shoulder-blade,

and finger and thumb
the parachute silk of his punctured lung.

Only then could I bind the struts
and climb the rungs of his broken ribs,

and feel the hurt
of his grazed heart.

Skirting along,
only then could I picture the scan,

the foetus of metal beneath his chest
where the bullet had finally come to rest.

Then I widened the search,
traced the scarring back to its source

to a sweating, unexploded mine
buried deep in his mind, around which

every nerve in his body had tightened and closed.
Then, and only then, did I come close.

*from* SEEING STARS

# The Christening

I am a sperm whale. I carry up to 2.5 tonnes of an oil-like balm in my huge, coffin-shaped head. I have a brain the size of a basketball, and on that basis alone am entitled to my opinions. I am a sperm whale. When I breathe in, the fluid in my head cools to a dense wax and I nosedive into the depths. My song, available on audiocassette and compact disc, is a comfort to divorcees, astrologists and those who have 'pitched the quavering canvas tent of their thoughts on the rim of the dark crater'. The oil in my head is of huge commercial value and has been used by NASA, for even in the galactic emptiness of deep space it does not freeze. I am attracted to the policies of the Green Party *on paper* but once inside the voting booth my hand is guided by an unseen force. Sometimes I vomit large chunks of ambergris. My brother, Jeff, owns a camping and outdoor clothing shop in the Lake District and is a recreational user of cannabis. Customers who bought books about me also bought *Do Whales Have Belly Buttons?* by Melvin Berger and street maps of Cardiff. In many ways I have *seen it all*. I keep no pets. Lying motionless on the surface I am said to be 'logging', and 'lobtailing' when I turn and offer my great slow fluke to the horizon. Don't be taken in by the dolphins and their winning smiles, they are the pickpockets of the ocean, the gypsy children of the open waters and they are laughing all the way to Atlantis. On the basis of 'finders keepers' I believe the Elgin Marbles should remain the property of the British Crown. I am my own God – why shouldn't I be? The first people to open me up thought my head was full of sperm, but they were men, and had lived without women for many weeks, and were far from home. Stuff comes blurting out.

# An Accommodation

—— and I both agreed that something had to change,
but I was still stunned and not a little hurt when I
staggered home one evening to find she'd draped a
net curtain slap bang down the middle of our home.
She said, 'I'm over here and you're over there, and
from now on that's how it's going to be.' It was a
small house, not much more than a single room,
which made for one or two practical problems.
Like the fridge was on my side and the oven was on
hers. And she had the bed while I slept fully
clothed in the inflatable chair. Also there was a
Hüsker Dü CD on her half of the border which I
wouldn't have minded hearing again for old times'
sake, and her winter coat stayed hanging on the
door in my domain. But the net was the net, and we
didn't so much as pass a single word through its
sacred veil, let alone send a hand crawling beneath
it, or, God forbid, yank it aside and go marching
across the line. Some nights she'd bring men back,
deadbeats, incompatible, not fit to kiss the heel of
her shoe. But it couldn't have been easy for her
either, watching me mooch about like a ghost,
seeing me crashing around in the empty bottles and
cans. And there were good times too, sitting side by
side on the old settee, the curtain between us, the
TV in her sector but angled towards me, taking me
into account.

Over the years the moths moved in, got a taste for
the net, so it came to resemble a giant web, like a

thing made of actual holes strung together by fine, nervous threads. But there it remained, and remains to this day, this tattered shroud, this ravaged lace suspended between our lives, keeping us inseparable and betrothed.

# I'll Be There to Love and Comfort You

The couple next door were testing the structural fabric
of the house with their difference of opinion. 'I can't
take much more of this,' I said to Mimi, my wife. Right
then there was another almighty crash, as if every pan
in the kitchen had clattered to the tiled floor. Mimi said,
'Try to relax. Take one of your tablets.' She brewed a
pot of camomile tea and we retired to bed. But the
pounding and caterwauling carried on right into the small
hours. I was dreaming that the mother of all asteroids
was locked on a collision course with planet Earth,
when unbelievably a fist came thumping through the
bedroom wall just above the headboard. In the metallic
light of the full moon I saw the bloody knuckles and a
cobweb tattoo on the flap of skin between finger and
thumb, before the fist withdrew. Mimi's face was
powdered with dirt and dust, but she didn't wake. She
looked like a corpse pulled from the rubble of an
earthquake after five days in a faraway country famous
only for its paper kites.

I peered through the hole in the wall. It was dark on the
other side, with just occasional flashes of purple or green
light, like those weird electrically powered life forms
zipping around in the ocean depths. There was a rustling
noise, like something stirring in a nest of straw, then a
voice, a voice no bigger than a sixpence, crying for help.
Now Mimi was right next to me. 'It's her,' she said. I
said, 'Don't be crazy, Mimi, she'd be twenty-four by
now.' 'It's her I tell you. Get her back, do you hear me?
GET HER BACK.' I rolled up my pyjama sleeve and

pushed my arm into the hole, first to my elbow, then as
far as my shoulder and neck. The air beyond was
clammy and damp, as if I'd reached into a nineteenth-century
London street in late November, fog rolling in up
the river, a cough in a doorway. Mimi was out of her
mind by now. My right cheek and my ear were flat to the
wall. Then slowly but slowly I opened my fist to the
unknown. And out of the void, slowly but slowly it
came: the pulsing starfish of a child's hand, swimming
and swimming and coming to settle on my upturned
palm.

# The English Astronaut

He splashed down in rough seas off Spurn Point.
I watched through a coin-op telescope jammed
with a lollipop stick as a trawler fished him out
of the waves and ferried him back to Mission
Control on a trading estate near the Humber Bridge.
He spoke with a mild voice: yes, it was good to be
home; he'd missed his wife, the kids, couldn't wait
for a shave and a hot bath. 'Are there any more
questions?' No, there were not.

I followed him in his Honda Accord to a Little
Chef on the A1, took the table opposite, watched
him order the all-day breakfast and a pot of tea.
'You need to go outside to do that,' said the
waitress when he lit a cigarette. He read the paper,
started the crossword, poked at the black pudding
with his fork. Then he stared through the window
for long unbroken minutes at a time, but only at the
busy road, never the sky. And his face was not the
moon. And his hands were not the hands of a man
who had held between finger and thumb the blue
planet, and lifted it up to his watchmaker's eye.

# Hop In, Dennis

A man was hitching a lift on the slip road of the A16 just outside Calais. Despite his sharp, chiselled features and a certain desperation to his body language, I felt compelled to pick him up, so I pulled across and rolled down the window. He stuck his face in the car and said, 'I am Dennis Bergkamp, player of football for Arsenal. Tonight we have game in Luxembourg but because I am fear of flying I am travel overland. Then I have big argument with chauffeur and here he drops me. Can you help?' 'Hop in, Dennis,' I said. He threw his kit in the back and buckled up next to me. 'So what was the barney about?' I asked him. Dennis sighed and shook his classical-looking head. 'He was ignoramus. He was dismissive of great Dutch master Vermeer and says Rembrandt was homosexual.' 'Well you'll hear no such complaints from me,' I assured him. We motored along and the landscape just zipped by. And despite some of the niggles and tetchiness which crept into Dennis's game during the latter part of his career, he was a perfect gentleman and the complete travelling companion. For example, he limited himself to no more than four wine gums from the bag which gaped open between us, and was witty and illuminating without ever resorting to name-dropping or dressing-room gossip.

Near the Belgian border a note of tiredness entered Dennis's voice, so to soothe him to sleep I skipped from Classic Rock to Easy Listening. It wasn't until we were approaching the outskirts of the city that he stirred and looked at his Rolex. 'It will sure be a tight one,' he said. 'Why don't you get changed in the car and I'll drop you

off at the ground?' I suggested. 'Good plan,' he said, and
wriggled into the back. In the corner of my eye he was a
contortion of red and white, like Santa Claus in a badger
trap, though of course I afforded him complete privacy,
because like most professionally trained drivers I use only
the wing mirrors, never the rear view. Pretty swiftly he
dropped into the seat beside me, being careful not to
scratch the console with his studs. 'Here's the stadium,' I
said, turning into a crowded boulevard awash with flags
and scarves. Dennis jogged away towards a turnstile,
through which the brilliance of the floodlights shone
like the light from a distant galaxy.

And it's now that I have to confess that Mr Bergkamp was
only one of dozens of Dennises to have found their way
into the passenger seat of my mid-range saloon. Denis
Healey, Dennis Hopper, Dennis Potter, Dennis Lillee, the
underrated record producer Dennis Bovell, and many,
many more. I once drove Denis Thatcher from Leicester
Forest East service station to Ludlow races and he wasn't a
moment's bother, though I did have to ask him to refrain
from smoking, and of course not to breathe one word about
the woman who introduced rabies to South Yorkshire.

# The Accident

Leo burnt his hand very badly on a jet of steam
which hissed from his toasted pitta bread as he
opened it up with a knife. The visiting nurse said,
'Are you sure you haven't been beating up your
wife?' 'Excuse me?' said Leo. 'Are you sure you
didn't sustain this injury during the course of
physically assaulting your wife?' questioned the
nurse. Leo was shocked. 'It's a burn,' he said.
'Of course it's a burn, but who's to say she
wasn't defending herself with a steam iron or a
frying pan? Do you cook your own meals, sir, or
do you insist on your wife doing the housework?'
Leo was flabbergasted. 'I'm not even married,'
he said. 'Yeah, right, and I'm the Angel of the
North,' she said, throwing him a roll of lint as she
barged out of the house and slammed the door
behind her.

Leo really wasn't married. His friends were
married. Both of them. One was even divorced.
But Leo was a bachelor and not at all happy with
the situation. Bachelor – the word tasted like
diesel in his mouth. However, that night in the
pub he met Jacqueline, a young blind woman
from York, and they talked for a while on the
subject of Easter Island, about which neither of
them knew anything, and after an hour they were
still talking, and a few moments later their knees
touched under the wooden table. For him it was
like a parachute opening. For her it was like

something involving an artichoke. He lifted his
hopelessly bandaged hand to within a millimetre
of her cheek and said, 'Jacqueline, I'll never hurt
you. I wouldn't do that. Everything's going to be
all right from now on and you're safe. Jackie, I
love you. Do you understand?'

# Aviators

They'd overbooked the plane. 'At this moment in time,'
announced the agent at the counter, 'Rainbow Airlines
is offering one hundred pounds or a free return flight to
any passenger willing to stand down.' A small man in a
cheap suit and Bart Simpson socks scratched his ankle.
'One hundred and fifty pounds,' she announced, fifteen
minutes later. Nobody moved. 'Two hundred?' From
nowhere, this neat-looking chap in a blue flannel jacket
and shiny shoes loomed over the desk and said, 'I'll take
the money.' 'But you're the pilot,' she said, then added,
'Sir,' as if she'd walked into a Japanese house and
forgotten to take off her shoes. The pilot whispered,
'Listen, I need that money. I'm behind on my mortgage
payments because my wife's a gambler. I've got two
sons at naval college – the hats alone cost a small fortune
– and I'm being blackmailed by a pimp in Stockport. Let
me take the two hundred, you'd be saving my life.'

I'd been sitting within earshot, next to the stand-up
ashtray. 'Give him the money,' I said. 'Who are you?'
asked Dorothy (she was wearing a plastic name-badge
with gold letters). 'Dorothy, I'm George,' I said, 'and
clearly this man's in pain. I don't want him going all
gooey midway over the English Channel. I once heard
sobbing coming from the cabin of a Jumbo Jet at thirty-three
thousand feet, and it sounded like the laughter of
Beelzebub.' 'But who'll fly the plane?' she wanted to
know. 'Why me, of course.' I opened my mouth so she
could see how good my teeth were – like pilot's teeth.
'Do you have a licence?' she asked. I said, 'Details,

always details. Dorothy, it's time to let go a little, to trust in the unexplained. Time to open your mind to the infinite.' By now my hand was resting on hers, and a small crowd of passengers had gathered around, nodding and patting me on the back. 'Good for you, George,' said a backpacker with a leather shoelace knotted around his wrist. It was biblical, or like the end of a family film during the time of innocence. I said, 'Dorothy, give me the keys to the cockpit, and let's get this baby in the air.'

# The Practical Way to Heaven

The opening of the new exhibition space at the Sculpture Farm had been a wonderful success. 'Would all those visitors returning to London on the 3:18 from Wakefield Westgate please make their way to the main entrance from where the shuttle bus is about to depart,' announced a nasaly Maggie over the PA system. She'd been having trouble with her adenoids. The London people put down their wine glasses and plates and began to move through the concourse. 'Great show, Jack,' said Preminger, helping himself to a final goat's cheese tartlet and a skewered Thai prawn. 'And not a pie in sight!' 'Thanks for coming,' said Jack. 'Put that somewhere for me, will you?' said Preminger, passing Jack his redundant cocktail stick before shaking hands and marching off towards the coach. A proud and happy man, Jack asked his staff, all eight of them, to assemble in the cafeteria, and he thanked them for their effort. 'Have all the Londoners gone?' he asked Maggie. 'Yes,' she said through her nose, peering out of the window as the back wheels of the bus rattled over the cattle grid. 'Very good. So here's your reward,' said Jack. He clapped his hands, and in through the double doors of the kitchen came Bernard driving a forklift truck, and on it, the most enormous pie. A wild, ecstatic cheer reverberated among the tables and chairs. 'Fill your wellies!' cried Jack. Tina from the gift shop could not restrain herself; she ripped off a section of the crust, dunked her arm in as far as her elbow, and smeared her face with rich brown gravy. Seth the gardener wasn't far behind, gnashing frenziedly at the crimped edging, followed by Millicent from publicity who hooked out a juicy piece of steak, went down on all fours and gorged on it like a starving dingo. Soon everyone was devouring the pie. And like all the great pies of history, the more they ate, the bigger it became. Jack threw his jacket into the corner of the room and whipped off his shirt and trousers. He was wearing blue swimming trunks. Standing on the rim of the metal dish he lowered himself through the light pastry topping. Maggie followed suit in her bra and pants, until all the staff of the Sculpture Farm were rolling or wading or lolling or lazing or helping themselves in the great slow pool of the pie. Now the forklift doubled as a diving board as Bernard bellyflopped from one of its prongs into the warm mush. It was only after retrieving a baby carrot from between his toes that Jack looked up and saw Preminger, who'd forgotten his wallet. 'You people,' he seethed. His face looked like the smell of a broken sewer in high summer. Jack stood up. 'I can explain everything,' he said. A chunk of braised celery slithered over his sternum. Preminger spluttered, 'You told me the pie thing was over. Finished. You said it was safe in the north, Jack Singleton. But look at you. Call yourself a Sculpture Farmer? You couldn't clean out a hamster cage.' 'Forgive us,' said Jack. 'We're pie people. Our mothers and fathers were pie people, and their mothers and fathers before them. Pies are in our blood.' 'Don't tell it to me. Tell it to them,' said Preminger, pointing to the window. On the other side of the glass stood the idling coach. Like a row of gargoyles, the faces of critics, sponsors, trustees, rich benefactors and famous names from the world of animal art looked out disgusted and appalled. Preminger swivelled on his heel and exited. The bus revved and departed.

Leaving gravy footprints behind him, Jack wandered out of the building and into the landscape beyond. And the crocodile of staff followed him, past the iron pigs, up to the granite bull on the hill, then along by the pit pony carved in coal and the shimmering flock of stainless steel geese in the far meadow. Finally they found themselves in a small temple in the woods, with tea lights on the stone steps, the flames of which looked like the sails from a flotilla of tiny yachts in a distant bay. Torches to each corner of the building burned with an imperial pride. In front of Jack, soaked in pie juice, stood his loyal staff: Jethro with his three fingers; Maggie with her shopping problem; Tina who'd fallen in a quarry; Conrad who'd done time. Jack said, 'In the horse I see the plough, in the bull I see the wheel, in the goat I see the scythe, in the pig I see the stove. Bernard,' he shouted into the shadowy woods behind them, 'bring out the custard.'

# Beyond Huddersfield

We drove a couple of hundred miles north. To sip beer in
a log cabin. To taste the air from the mountains and feel
the DNA of our ancestors tingle in our marrow. We
hooked compliant fish from the lake, grilled them over a
log fire and ate with our hands as the sun melted into the
west. And on leaving, we left the place just as we'd found
it: cleaned out the stove, swept the veranda, made a
fingertip search of the meadow for the tiniest slivers of
silver foil and suchlike, and folded the cold ashes into the
earth. On the way south we pulled in at a roadside
recycling site to offload the rubbish. The woman on the
gate with the gun and the clipboard waved us over and said,
'Plastics in one, cans in two, cardboard and paper in three,
and there's a bear in four, so mind how you go.' True
enough, in the last skip, a black bear was squatting in a pile
of junk. He was a sizeable creature and no mistake, could
have creamed my head clean off with one swipe of those
claws had the notion occurred. But he just sat there, on his
throne of trash, doing nothing, staring his five-mile stare.

In the days that followed I thought a lot about that bear.
With every recollection he became more wretched and
undignified in my mind, and I couldn't suppress the
escalation of inglorious imagery. First he was begging with
a paper cup. The next time I thought about him he was
wearing a nylon housecoat. Then a pair of Ugg boots, and
the tortilla wrap between his paws was a soiled nappy.
Then he was flipping burgers with a floral lampshade on
his head and a whitewall tyre around his neck, and the next
weekend, either for his sake or mine, nothing could stop me

jumping in the car after work and racing north to the tip. It was two in the morning when I drew up. The gate was locked but I hopped over, walked onto the gantry above the dumping bays and shone a torch into the void. There he was, asleep in the skip, snoring like a sawmill. But swinging the car around to drive home the headlights made one final sweep of the scene, and I saw him again, on his hind legs now, the grapefruit in his mouth like a luminous gumshield, pizza toppings and chicken bones hanging from his matted coat, a red bandana knotted tightly around his skinny thigh, leaning to his work, busy at his groin, the gleaming needle digging for the sunken vein.

# The Delegates

At the annual Conference of Advanced Criminal Psychology,
Dr Amsterdam and myself skipped the afternoon seminar on
Offending Behaviours Within Gated Communities and went
into town to go nicking stuff. In Halfords he pilfered a shiny
aluminium gizmo for measuring the tread depth on a car tyre
and I nabbed a four-digit combination lock. In the gardening
section of John Lewis's he filched a Butterflies of the British
Countryside Wallchart while I pocketed a squirrel-proof bird
feeder. In Poundstretcher he whipped a small tin of Magic
Stain Remover and I helped myself to a signed 2005 official
McFly calendar. In Specsavers he purloined a pair of silver-
rimmed varifocals and I lifted an origami snowflake from the
window display. In Waterstone's he slipped an unauthorised
biography of disgraced South African cricket captain Hansie
Cronje inside his raincoat and I sneaked out with an Original
Magnetic Poetry Kit. In Oxfam he appropriated a five-
hundred-piece Serengeti at Dusk jigsaw and I swiped a set of
six coasters designed by authenticated aborigines. Then with
our laminated delegate passes streaming over our shoulders
on lanyards of pink and purple ribbon we legged it out of the
precinct and across the park. And from the high iron bridge
we slung the lot over the ornate railings into the filthy river
below until every last item of merchandise had either sunk
without trace or was drifting away downstream. 'Remind
me, Stephen, why we do this,' said Dr Amsterdam. I said,
'I really don't recall.' Peeling a brown calfskin glove from
the cold, moulded fingers of his prosthetic hand he said,
'Let's make this our last, shall we?' We shook on the deal,
and even managed a partial embrace. A mute swan pecked
idly at a Paisley-patterned chiffon scarf before it picked up
speed and slithered over the weir.

## Last Day on Planet Earth

Lippincott takes a photograph with his eye.
Wittmann paints in the crust of salt with a
finger of spit. Yoshioka wheels the last
piano onto the fire. Owens throws stones at
a rock. The afternoon turns over in its sleep,
then sleeps.

Kirszenstein trades her kingfisher skull for
a tinned peach. Jerome traps air in a screw-top
jar. Bambuck plants the last of his teeth.
Johnson dresses his gangrenous wound with
a carrier bag. Bolt pulls up the ladder,
secures the hatch.

*from* BLACK ROSES:
THE KILLING OF SOPHIE LANCASTER

(It was one small step
across the street
but one giant leap
into bed-sit land,
and very grown up
to be moving in,
to be given the keys,
to lift the latch,
to be playing house,
to be lady and lord
of our very own place,
in our very own space.

We were dreamers, asleep.
We were jobless, skint,
always juggling
and having to stint,
not a cent to our name,
always struggling
to make ends meet,
to eke things out
till the end of the week.
Never enough
to save or spend,
always a case
of make do and mend.
Couldn't afford
a lick of paint,

kitted it out
with sticks of furniture
borrowed and begged,
splashed each wall
with home-made art,
insulated the hall with books.
We were suddenly dish-washers,
bed-makers, fire-lighters, cooks.

To the passer-by
it was hardly The Ritz,
nowhere to shout
or show off about,
just some old, cold
first-floor flat
below the moor,
above a shop,
but to us it was home,
palace and penthouse,
fortress and funhouse,
studio, library
all rolled into one.
We could bolt the door
and keep the world out
or watch the world
as it wandered past,
in all its glory, beautifully mad,

all the nightshift workers and daylight shirkers,
the mods and rockers and emos and moshers
and joggers and bikers and slackers and slickers,

all the swimmers and sinkers and grafters and thinkers,
all the fly-posters and bill-stickers,
the goths and the straights and the groovers and ravers,
the movers and shakers, the candlestick makers . . .
all the pissheads and potheads and veggies and vegans
and coppers and preachers and posties and traders,
the night-hawks and the dawn-treaders,
the speed-freaks and the metal-merchants,
the scrimpers and savers, the beggars and trail-blazers,
all the chancers and mystics and givers and takers,

the skinheads and suedeheads and non-believers,
all the tattooed crusties, all the crested Mohicans,
all the folkies and rappers and ragamuffins
and rastas and clubbers and dubbers and mixers
and suited commuters and duckers and divers
and salesmen and truckers and lollipop ladies
and beatniks and peaceniks and streetkids and skaters
and hitchers and drivers and runners and riders,
all the rat-racers and the money servants,
all the dancers and deejays,
all the trippers and heavies and slackers and hippies
and hawkers and vendors and takers and lenders
and the dog-walkers and the dawdlers,
all the late starters and the early risers . . .

all the human race
in its crazy parade.

I said let them all be.
I said breathe and let breathe.)

*from* THE DEATH OF KING ARTHUR

The Monarch was on his mighty boat with many men,
enclosed in a cabin among copious equipment.
And while resting on a richly arrayed bed
he was soothed to sleep by the swaying of the sea.
And he dreamed of a dragon dreadful to behold
that came darting over the deep to drown his people,
arrowing directly from the regions of the west
and swooping with menace over the sea's wide span.
His head and neck were hooded all over
with hazy azure, enamelled in bright hues.
His shoulders were shawled in shining silver
so the serpent was shielded by steely scales.
His wings and his womb were wondrously coloured
and in his marvellous mail he mounted the heavens.
His tail was tasselled with bladed tongues
so what fellows it touched were fatally felled.
His feet were furred in the finest sable
and his cruel claws were encased in pure gold.
So furious were the flames that flowed from his lips
that the sea itself seemed to seethe with fire.
Then out of the east, to oppose him head-on,
from above the clouds came a brutish black bear,
huge paws and pads on the pillars of his legs
with pinion-sharp claws, curved in appearance.
Hateful and hideous were his hairs and everything:
his legs were bandy and lagged with bushy bristles
all muddy and matted, and he foamed at the mouth,
the foulest figure that was ever formed.
He went barrelling about with a bellicose look,
readying those raking claws for the clash.

He let rip with such a roar that the whole earth reeled,
striking out bloodily as he bullocked into battle.
Then the dragon in the distance dived straight for him,
and chased him through the sky with challenges and charges,
flying and fighting with the focus of a falcon.
He attacked with both fire and talons in tandem,
but the bear grew bigger and bolder in battle,
gouging flesh with his fearful fangs.
He caused such cuts with those cruel claws
that his breast and belly poured with blood,
and his blows were so crashing they cracked the earth's crust
and rivers ran red with crimson rain.
His strength alone might have laid low that lizard
were it not for the flames which he fired in defence.
The serpent ascended to the sky's ceiling,
then stooped steeply through the clouds and struck,
attacked with his talons and tore his back
which was ten foot in length from top to tail,
till the last living breath was beaten from that bear –
let him fall in the flood and float where it flows.
In his cabin, so disturbed was the King by those creatures
he nearly burst with the burden on the bed where he lay.

*from* IN MEMORY OF WATER
*(Stanza Stones)*

# Snow

The sky has delivered
its blank missive.
The moor in coma.
Snow, like water asleep,
a coded muteness
to baffle all noise,
to stall movement,
still time.
What can it mean
that colourless water
can dream
such depth of white?
We should make the most
of the light.

Stars snag
on its crystal points.
The odd, unnatural pheasant
struts and slides.
Snow, snow, snow
is how the snow speaks,
is how its clean page reads.
Then it wakes, and thaws,
and weeps.

# Rain

Be glad
of these freshwater tears,
each pearled droplet
some salty old sea-bullet
air-lifted out of the waves,
then laundered and sieved,
recast as a soft bead
and returned.

And no matter how much
it strafes or sheets,
it is no mean feat
to catch one raindrop
clean in the mouth,
to take one drop
on the tongue, tasting
cloud-pollen,
grain of the heavens,
raw sky.

Let it teem, up here
where the front of the mind
distils
the brunt of the world.

# Mist

Who does it mourn?
What does it mean,
such nearness,
gathering here
on high ground
while your back was turned,
drawing its net curtains around?
Featureless silver screen, mist
is water
in its ghost state,
all inwardness,
holding its milky breath,
veiling the pulsing machines
of great cities
under your feet,
walling you
into these moments,
into this anti-garden
of gritstone and peat.

Given time
the edge of your being
will seep
into its fibreless fur;
you are lost, adrift
in hung water and blurred air,
but you are here.

# Dew

The tense stand-off
of summer's end,
the touchy fuse-wire
of parched grass,
tapers of bulrush and reed,
any tree
a primed mortar
of tinder, one spark
enough to trigger
a march on the moor
by ranks of flame.

Dew enters the field
under cover of night,
tending the weary and sapped,
lifting its thimble of drink
to the lips of a leaf,
to the stoat's tongue,
trimming a length of barbed-wire fence
with liquid gems, here
where bog-cotton
flags its surrender
or carries its torch
for the rain.

Then dawn, when sunrise
plants its fire-star
in each drop, ignites
each trembling eye.

## Puddle

Rain-junk.
Sky-litter.
Some May mornings
Atlantic storm-horses
clatter this way,
shedding their iron shoes
in potholes and ruts,
shoes that melt
into steel-grey puddles
then settle and set
into cloudless mirrors
by noon.

The shy deer
of the daytime moon
comes to sip from the rim.
But the sun
likes the look of itself,
stares all afternoon,
its hard eye
lifting the sheen
from the glass,
turning the glaze
to rust.
Then we don't see things
for dust.

# Beck

It is all one chase.
Trace it back: the source
might be nothing more
than a teardrop
squeezed from a curlew's eye,
then follow it down
to the full-throated roar
at its mouth:
a dipper
strolls the river
dressed for dinner
in a white bib.

The unbroken thread
of the beck
with its nose for the sea,
all flux and flex,
soft-soaping a pebble
for thousands of years,
or here
after hard rain
sawing the hillside in half
with its chain.
Or here,
where water unbinds
and hangs
at the waterfall's face,
and just for that one
stretched white moment
becomes lace.

*from* THE UNACCOMPANIED

# Poundland

Came we then to the place abovementioned,
crossed its bristled threshold through robotic glass doors,
entered its furry heat, its flesh-toned fluorescent light.
Thus with wire-wrought baskets we voyaged,
and some with trolleys, back wheels flipping like trout tails,
cruised the narrow canyons twixt cascading shelves,
the prow of our journeying cleaving stale air.
Legion were the items that came tamely to hand:
five stainless steel teaspoons, ten corn-relief plasters,
the Busy Bear pedal bin liners fragranced with country lavender,
the Disney design calendar and diary set, three cans of Vimto,
cornucopia of potato-based snacks and balm for a sweet tooth,
toys and games, goods of Orient made, and of Cathay,
all under the clouded eye of CCTV,
beyond the hazard cone where serious chutney spillage had
    occurred.
Then emerged souls: the duty manager with a face like
    Doncaster,
mumbling, 'For so much, what shall we give in return?'
The blood-stained employee of the month,
sobbing on a woolsack of fun-fur rugs,
many uniformed servers, spectral, drifting between aisles.
Then came Elpenor, our old friend Elpenor,
slumped and shrunken by the Seasonal Products display.
In strangled words I managed,
'How art thou come to these shady channels, into hell's ravine?'
And he: '*To loan sharks I owe/the bone and marrow of my all.*'
Then Walt Whitman, enquiring politely of the delivery boy.
And from Special Occasions came forth Tiresias,
dead in life, alive in death, cider-scented and sock-less,

Oxfam-clad, shaving cuts to both cheeks, quoting the stock
    exchange.
And my own mother reaching out, slipping a tin of stewing
    steak
to the skirt pocket of her wedding dress,
blessed with a magician's touch, practised in need.

But never until the valley widened at the gated brink
did we open our lips to fish out those corn-coloured coins,
those minted obols, hard-won tokens graced with our
    monarch's head,
kept hidden beneath the tongue's eel, blood-tasting,
both ornament and safeguard, of armour made.
And paid forthwith, then broke surface
and breathed extraordinary daylight into starved lungs,
steered for home through precincts and parks scalded by
    polar winds,
laden with whatnot, lightened of golden quids.

# Harmonium

The Farrand Chapelette was gathering dust
in the shadowy porch of Marsden Church.
And was due to be bundled off to the skip.
Or was mine, for a song, if I wanted it.

Sunlight, through stained glass, which on bright days
might beatify saints or raise the dead,
had aged the harmonium's softwood case
and yellowed the fingernails of its keys.
And one of its notes had lost its tongue,
and holes were worn in both the treadles
where the organist's feet, in grey, woollen socks
and leather-soled shoes, had pedalled and pedalled.

But its hummed harmonics still struck a chord:
for a hundred years that organ had stood
by the choristers' stalls, where father and son,
each in their time, had opened their throats
and gilded finches – like high notes – had streamed out.

Through his own blue cloud of tobacco smog,
with smoker's fingers and dottled thumbs,
he comes to help me cart it away.
And we carry it flat, laid on its back.
And he, being him, can't help but say
that the next box I'll shoulder through this nave
will bear the freight of his own dead weight.
And I, being me, then mouth in reply
some shallow or sorry phrase or word
too starved of breath to make itself heard.

# Paper Aeroplane

The man sitting next to me on the flight
was reading a blank book, keen eyes
panning left to right across empty leaves, fingers
turning from one white space to the next.

Sometimes he'd nod agreeably or shake his head,
or painstakingly underline some invisible text
with red ink, or decorate the margin
with an exclamation mark or asterisk.

It was a hefty-looking tome, hand-stitched
but wordless front and back and down the spine.
Coming in to land he laid the silver ribbon-marker
between two bare pages to save his place.

I was wearing noise-cancelling headphones,
listening to fine mist, when he leaned across
and shouted, 'Forgive the intrusion, but
would you sign this for me? I think it's your best.'